PSYCHOANALYTIC
Approaches for Counselors

THEORIES FOR COUNSELORS SERIES

Psychoanalytic Approaches for Counselors

Frederick Redekop
Kutztown University of Pennsylvania

PSYCHOANALYTIC
Approaches for Counselors

Frederick Redekop
Kutztown University of Pennsylvania

Los Angeles | London | New Delhi
Singapore | Washington DC

Los Angeles | London | New Delhi
Singapore | Washington DC

FOR INFORMATION:

SAGE Publications, Inc.
2455 Teller Road
Thousand Oaks, California 91320
E-mail: order@sagepub.com

SAGE Publications Ltd.
1 Oliver's Yard
55 City Road
London, EC1Y 1SP
United Kingdom

SAGE Publications India Pvt. Ltd.
B 1/I 1 Mohan Cooperative Industrial Area
Mathura Road, New Delhi 110 044
India

SAGE Publications Asia-Pacific Pte. Ltd.
3 Church Street
#10–04 Samsung Hub
Singapore 049483

Acquisitions Editor: Kassie Graves
Editorial Assistant: Carrie Montoya
Production Editor: Kelly DeRosa
Copy Editor: Deanna Noga
Typesetter: Hurix Systems Pvt. Ltd.
Proofreader: Theresa Kay
Indexer: Maria Sosnowski
Cover Designer: Anuparma Krishnan
Marketing Manager: Shari Countryman

Printed in the United States of America

Library of Congress Cataloging-in-Publication Data

Redekop, Frederick.

Psychoanalytic approaches for counselors / Frederick Redekop, Kutztown University of Pennsylvania.

pages cm.—(Theories for counselors series ; volume 1)

Includes bibliographical references and index.

ISBN 978-1-4522-6836-1 (pbk.)

1. Counseling. 2. Psychoanalysis. I. Title.

BF636.6.R433 2014

150.19'5—dc23 2014020166

This book is printed on acid-free paper.

SFI label applies to text stock

14 15 16 17 18 10 9 8 7 6 5 4 3 2 1

Brief Contents

Table of Contents

Series Preface

"Theories for Counselors" provides practical applications of major theories from a common factors, multicultural perspective. What does that mean? Let's break it down.

The authors in the "Theories for Counselors" series are highly experienced counselors with extensive knowledge and expertise concerning the theory that they present. They present each theory from an applied perspective, asking themselves, "How is this concept useful in actual clinical practice?" It may surprise you to know this, but Freud's work can be (and is) applied day in and day out in modern counseling. (If this surprises you, it could indicate that you have not been taught Freud well.) He believed that the relationship between the client and clinician was of utmost importance; he believed that his patients needed to feel comfortable speaking their mind; he believed that clinicians needed to listen with attentiveness and tact. Freud's legacy, as will be shown in the first book of this series, *Psychoanalytic Approaches for Counselors,* has been revised and revisited, but its therapeutic usefulness remains, and for each theory that is presented, therapeutic utility is utmost on the minds of the authors as they present material to their readers.

Each book begins by addressing the two most vital themes common to any counseling theory: the client and the therapeutic relationship. Why have we picked the client and the therapeutic relationship as the two most important themes? The reason is called the *common factors hypothesis,* and this is where research comes in. The common factors hypothesis is the result of decades of research that has compared various schools of counseling and psychotherapy. Contrary to prior belief, it has been convincingly demonstrated that research in general finds no significant difference in how effective the various therapies are. These findings, predicted by Rosenzweig (1936) nearly 80 years ago, began to be empirically demonstrated in the mid-1970s (Luborsky, Singer, & Luborsky, 1975; Smith & Glass, 1977). Research confirming the relative equivalence of bona fide therapies has accumulated since that time (e.g., Ahn & Wampold, 2001; Lambert &

Barley, 2001; Lambert & Ogles, 2004; Wampold, Mondin, Moody, Stich, Benson, & Ahn, 1997).

What does this mean? It means that instead of therapeutic improvement being due to specific ingredients prescribed by different theoretical schools of counseling and psychotherapy, positive therapeutic change can be attributed to factors that are common to all bona fide therapies. Additionally, these factors can be broken down into four categories: (1) Client variables (40% of change); (2) Relationship variables (30%); (3) Hope/expectancy (15%), and (4) Theory or technique (15%) (Duncan, 2002; Lambert, 1992) (see Figure 1).

As we see, the client and the relationship accounts for the vast majority of therapeutic change, and as such, should be centrally located in the presentation of any counseling theory.

Interestingly, the history of counseling begins right where research predicts: In an intense relationship between one person who wants help and another person wanting to help. Sigmund Freud, who inaugurated themes that continue to organize the counseling profession, described and redescribed the origins of psychoanalysis. Two major components in his descriptions were the famous first patient of psychoanalysis, Bertha Pappenheim (referred to in case studies as "Anna O.") and the relationship she had with her doctor, Josef Breuer, Freud's friend and colleague at the time. Though Freud revised his opinions on many things about that famous case (as he did about almost everything), what remained constant was the fact that he

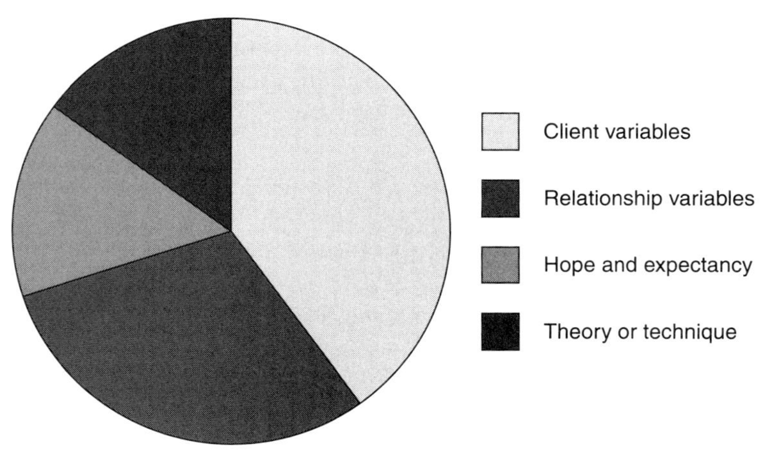

Figure 1 Common Factors

Lambert, M. J. (1992). Psychotherapy outcome research: Implications for integrative and eclectic therapists. In J. C. Norcross & M. R. Goldfried (Eds.), *Handbook of psychotherapy and behavior change* (4th ed., pp. 143–189). New York, NY: John Wiley.

saw something of primary importance in that case—the "talking cure" that occurs between a patient/client and doctor/counselor.

Thus the origins of counseling display a deep consonance with the latest in empirical research, and it is this consonance that is the underlying theme behind the series, "Theories for Counselors." Starting with Freud and moving through past and contemporary counseling theories and theorists, the focus remains on the client and the therapeutic relationship and how this relationship fosters and enhances the client's natural resilience and hope for change. The theory's techniques and the theory itself are important only inasmuch as they provide a common roadmap—a way for both client and counselor to think about where a client has been and where he or she wants to go.

Just as it is important to know that Freud remains useful for contemporary counselors, so it is important to know that Freud began his work against a backdrop of rising racial hatred in Austria and Western Europe and that while he successfully fled to England in 1938, his sisters perished in the Nazi concentration camps during the Holocaust (Gay, 2006). Thus the counseling enterprise began at a time of extreme racial hatred, which is a sobering and important fact to reflect on; from the inception of counseling in Western Europe and throughout its development worldwide, multicultural awareness and respect for diversity are no mere add-ons, but are integral components for the practice of counseling. In addition, another important group membership—gender—has assumed greater and greater importance in the counseling field; its central importance imbued the case of Bertha Pappenheim, which has been deemed the founding one for psychoanalysis and hence for all that followed.

Counselors must practice from a culturally aware place rather than one that would seek to downplay the impact of race, gender, and other important group affiliations on our clients' lives. Sue, Arrendo, and McDavis (1992) provided a conceptual framework for organizing the types of competencies needed by a culturally skilled counselor, saying that he or she becomes aware of his or her own assumptions, actively attempts to understand differing worldviews, and actively develops culturally sensitive intervention strategies and skills. Sue (2001) expanded his conceptual framework into a multidimensional model of cultural competence; this model was primarily focused on racial and ethnic minority groups, though he did also recognize that it might be applicable for other groups including those of "gender, sexual orientation, and ability/disability" (p. 816). Such topics are now recognized as rightfully fitting within the context of multicultural counseling (Conyers, 2002; Pope, 2002; Richardson & Jacob, 2002). In addition, Smith and Richards (2002) point out the obligation that counselors have to address issues of religion and spirituality as multicultural issues.

D'Andrea and Daniels (2001) provided a multicultural framework for working with clients that is RESPECTFUL and inclusive of: Religion and spirituality, Economic class, Sexual identity, Psychological development, Ethnic/racial identity, Chronology, Trauma, Family, Unique physical abilities and disabilities, and Language and location of residence. Similarly, Hays (2008) outlined a model that emphasized nine cultural influences in relation to specific minority groups that counselors should be "ADDRESSING": (1) Age, (2) Developmental and other, (3) Disabilities, (4) Religion, (5) Ethnicity/race, (6) Social status, (7) Sexual orientation, (8) Indigenous heritage, and (9) Gender. These models help counselors deliver diversity competent services and pay attention to all the potential resources that a client brings to the counseling encounter. Ultimately, respect for diversity and celebration of all aspects of culture and group membership should lead to a more nuanced understanding of the client and the sometimes-hidden strengths that he or she possesses. Better knowing a client enhances the richly relational counseling encounter that began with Freud's work.

Once again, this is consonant with the common factors approach. The common factors approach can be applied to, and makes sense of, any counseling theory, beginning with Freud and psychoanalysis. According to this approach, all bona fide counseling theories do the same thing, though they describe it using differing terminology. One analogy is traveling to a particular destination, say New York City. There is no one right way to get there—it depends on where you are starting from, whether you want to fly, drive, take the train, or whether you want to get there by a direct route or take a scenic one. Each unique route is analogous to a different counseling theory. The destination is the same—in a travel scenario, getting to New York City, and in a counseling scenario, achieving positive treatment outcome.

A BRIEF PRIMER ON THE COMMON FACTORS: HYPOTHESIS

- Suspecting that there were characteristics that all effective therapies (and therapists) shared, Rosenzweig (1936) makes the claim that there are common factors upon which good counseling rests, regardless of theoretical orientation.
- Researching further, scholars use meta-analysis—a summary about relevant empirical studies or an "analysis of analyses"—as a tool to compare treatment outcome studies.
- Gaining consensus from these meta-analytic studies, researchers suggest that positive therapeutic treatment outcome is due to the following 4 groups of factors:

1. Client/extratherapeutic factors: 40%
2. Therapeutic relationship factors: 30%

3. Placebo/expectancy for change/hope: 15%
4. Theory/technique: 15%
(Duncan, 2002)

- Correcting the above breakdown, later researchers suggest that while the common factors hypothesis has been supported—"these shared, curative factors drive the engine of therapy" (Hubble, Duncan, Miller, & Wampold, 2010, p. 28)—it has been somewhat oversimplified. The factors aren't discrete, but are complexly interrelated.
- Focusing on effective therapists rather than effective therapies should be emphasized, since there are large differences in effectiveness among clinicians; and "Using formal client feedback to inform, guide, and evaluate treatment is the strongest recommendation" that came from a comprehensive update of common factors (Hubble et al., 2010, p. 424).
- Condensing this into a sentence, it means that from a common factors perspective, counselors use a theoretical roadmap—i.e., employing language that makes sense to the client—that helps activate dormant client resources and enhance client hope and expectancy for change, within the context of a therapeutic relationship that "is characterized by trust, warmth, understanding, acceptance, kindness, and human wisdom" (Lambert & Ogles, 2004, p. 181) and that can allow for modifications and changes based on feedback from the client.

In their book, *The Heroic Client,* Duncan and Miller (2000) put it this way—they seek to "1) enhance those factors across theories that account for successful outcome; 2) encourage the client's unique integration of different theories; and 3) selectively apply diverse ideas and techniques as they are seen as relevant by the client" (p. 146). Miller has talked about the need for clinicians to know different theories because they serve as language resources to connect with the client. In this view, theory is a way to connect with clients; if one language that I'm using—for instance, solution focus therapy—doesn't appear to be the language that the client is speaking, then I should use other theoretical languages that might allow me to communicate better with my client. The test of theory is in how well it accords with each individual client's culturally influenced worldview and how useful it proves to be in the context of the therapeutic encounter.

"Theories for Counselors" will help you consider theories from the perspective of the client and what makes sense to her or him. It will show that theory and technique are good inasmuch as they aid clients in understanding their present situation and what they need to do to improve it. Finally, the series will help you situate the work of counseling within a sociocultural framework that takes into account client uniqueness, universality, and important group affiliations to enhance and activate client resources.

In the text that follows, I make frequent reference to Freud's *Five Lectures on Psycho-analysis*. This book, like many of Freud's, has been reprinted in a relatively inexpensive edition taken from the *Standard Edition of the Complete Psychological Works of Sigmund Freud,* and I highly recommend it as a companion to *Psychoanalytic Approaches for Counselors*. Freud presented the history of psychoanalysis many times throughout his career; I have found *Five Lectures* to be the best summary for students and regularly assign it as the primary source text from Freud's work in my classes.

I direct the reader to the companion website for this book and series, http://study.sagepub.com/theoriesforcounselors. There you will find extended discussions of topics that are mentioned briefly in the text, topics that are not addressed in the text but that might be useful to know when studying for comprehensive or licensing exams, definitions of terms, and supplemental exercises and activities. In general, if a topic is not covered or is covered in detail in the printed text, please search the website, because it will in all likelihood be discussed there.

Acknowledgments

Psychoanalytic Approaches for Counselors grew from my attempts in counseling theories classes to articulate to students the role of theory in our work with clients; I thank the many students whom I have had the privilege to work with for their helpful feedback and suggestions over the years.

I would like to thank the reviewers of this book for their many helpful comments and suggestions: Cecile Brennan, John Carroll University; Frank Malone, Philadelphia School of Psychoanalysis; Linda Thompson, Holy Family University; Jerome Wagner, Loyola University; and Kurt Kraus, Shippensburg University of Pennsylvania. I thank reviewers of the proposal for the "Theories for Counselors" series: Mike Hauser, University of Tennessee at Chattanooga; James W. Lichtenberg, University of Kansas; Kathryn C. MacCluskie, Cleveland State University; Judith Kaufman, PhD, Fairleigh Dickinson University; Dilani Perera-Diltz, Cleveland State University; Tara S. Jungersen, Nova Southeastern University; Michael R. McFee, Eastern University; Esteban Cardemil, Clark University; Walter Buboltz, Louisiana Tech University; and Mary C. Burke, Carlow University.

I extend special thanks to Chad Luke, Tennessee Tech University; Brian Pickell, and Madeleine Langman. Finally, I would like to thank Kassie Graves, publisher for SAGE's book program in the Human Services, for her skillful support in making this book and series a reality.

For Sallie and Ria

Introduction

I am not interested in converting anyone to Freudianism or glorifying Freud as a genius. As the title of this book suggests, my aim is to make psychoanalysis—Freud's ideas and clinical practices, along with later developments by those who followed in his footsteps—useful for counselors and counselors-in-training. Freud and his followers for counselors, not counselors for—or against—Freud. When we take a fresh look at Freud, a look predicated on the idea that Freud should be studied not simply for historical or polemical interest but for use and applicability, we find that we can construct broad themes, identify recurring clinical issues, and gain a larger perspective both on Freud's work and on contemporary clinical practice. Approached in this fashion, we can increase our clinical knowledge and avoid becoming overwhelmed with the complexity of his ideas or the daunting scholarship on Freud and psychoanalysis that has accumulated over the years.

In *Psychoanalytic Approaches for Counselors,* we begin by taking a brief look at Freud's life and historical context. We then consider the therapeutic themes that Freud inaugurated and review his achievements in light of the common factors hypothesis. In Chapter 1, The Talking Cure, we see that from the very beginning, the psychoanalytic relationship focused on the client. We find that this relationship is not just the container for therapeutic interventions, it is the most potent treatment intervention itself. In Chapter 2, Basic Psychoanalytic Concepts, we look at how Freud thought of our mental life as continuous struggle; in his view, the rational Ego attempts to mediate between unacceptable wishes and urges, internalized parental voices, and real-life demands of the external world. In Chapter 3, The Evolution of Psychoanalysis, we see that psychoanalysis continued to grow and evolve beyond Freud. Psychoanalysis moved from an internal, one-person drive model to a two- and more-person relational model and has integrated neuroscientific findings into its clinical theory and practice. In Chapter 4, Multiculturalism, we address three major multicultural categories, (1) race/ethnicity, (2) social class, and (3) sex/gender, and find that multicultural considerations have informed counseling from its inception in anti-Semitic Europe during Freud's life. We find that psychoanalysis, derided by some as a treatment only for the wealthy, in fact contains relational resources for work with all clients. In Chapter 5, A Case Illustration of Contemporary Psychoanalytic Counseling, we examine the fictitious case example of Jennie Lin. This case example illustrates some of the twists and turns that might occur in contemporary psychoanalytical practice as clients are encouraged to access insights that are dynamic and that can be rationally acted on. In Chapter 6, Conclusion, we summarize the major points of the book in service of the overarching aim of the *Theories for Counselors* series, which is to help us understand the contributions of each major theorist from a common factors perspective.

Who Was Sigmund Freud?

Freud was born on May 6, 1856, to a Jewish merchant, Jacob Freud, and his wife, Amalia, in what is now the Czech Republic town of Příbor (Freiberg). His family moved to Vienna in March of 1860, when Freud was nearing 4 years of age. Freud lived in Vienna most of his life, studying and working in a European city that was cosmopolitan and sophisticated yet deeply riven by racist attitudes. While there were promising strains of liberalization in culture and in politics, there were other more threatening tones and undertones in the political and social discourse in which Freud grew up and lived. As Gay (2006) demonstrates, the 19th century in Europe and in Vienna was "an uneasy interlude between the old anti-Semitism and the new" (p. 20). While there was much more opportunity available to Freud, scholastically and career-wise, there were also continued hints and threats of posts and advancement denied because of anti-Semitism.

Freud thus grew up in a complex social environment, an environment that promised shining advancement and murky threat. His family was also complex. Freud was the eldest of Jacob and Amalia's seven children; in addition to his siblings, Freud also had a number of half-siblings, since his father had two wives before he married Freud's mother. Freud's father was 20 years older than his mother, which was a puzzle to Freud as a child—why was his young and beautiful mother married to such an old fellow? The two sons from Jacob's first marriage lived nearby; one of Freud's nephew's was older than Freud was, and his half-brother Philipp seemed to be a much better romantic fit, age-wise, with his mother. It was all very confusing for Freud, and we might suspect that some of his early bemusement played a powerful role in his subsequent theorizing about mothers, fathers, and boys.

Throughout his academic career, Freud was a hardworking and gifted student. He enrolled in medicine at Vienna University and graduated with his medical degree in 1881. He met and fell in love with his future wife, Martha Bernays, in April of 1882 when he was in his mid-twenties; they were too poor to marry immediately. In 1885, Freud studied in Paris under the famous Jean-Martin Charcot and soon thereafter opened his private practice and married. Of particular note throughout the 1880s and 1890s were Freud's connections with Wilhelm Fliess and Josef Breuer, two colleagues with whom he shared intense personal and professional relationships.

With *The Interpretation of Dreams* (it came out in November of 1899 but bore the date of 1900), Freud published the first major text of psychoanalysis. While Freud used the word *psychoanalysis* earlier in 1896 in French and German (Gay, 2006), and had developed his theory before its publication, *The Interpretation of Dreams* began an avalanche of lectures, papers, and books in which Freud articulated his mature views. In text after text on sexuality, on therapeutic technique, and on psychology and metapsychology, Freud provided the world with intriguing evidence that "the mind, however disheveled it might appear, is governed by firm rules" (Gay, 1989a, p. xvi). Freud was a tireless worker and advocate for psychoanalysis, presiding over meetings, writing letters, maintaining professional relationships, and indefatigably advancing the cause of psychoanalysis until his death on September 23, 1939, shortly after France and Britain declared war on Germany.

In considering Freud's life, it is important to keep in mind Gay's (2006) reminder that while he entertained the most scandalous of ideas, he was a proper bourgeois, regulated by work and by the clock. Freud would rise in the morning at seven, seeing clients from eight to twelve. Dinner, with the full household assembled, took place at one, followed by a walk. Consultations began at three, followed by more patients. Supper might take place as late as nine, followed by cards, or a walk or trip to a café; following this, he would read, write, and edit articles. At the end of this long day, he would go to bed at one in the morning. He was also devoted to his family, spending time with them at meals and during their summer family vacations. His devotion was poignantly illustrated in the grief and sorrow he felt over the losses suffered by his family (such as the death of his daughter, Sophie, and his grandson, Heinz); Freud, who came to see life as a war between the forces of life—Eros—and death—Thanatos—was a human being who deeply experienced both in his long life.

The Relevance of Psychoanalysis

This brief synopsis introduces us to the historical Freud, but it nowhere addresses his relevance. It is my contention that textbooks and classes on Freud often do a relatively good job of describing Freud's historical significance and the architecture of his system—as if it were some interesting cathedral wherein esoteric and sometimes cruel rites were once carried out—but a relatively poor job of describing his contemporary significance. Through my own experience working with clients, talking with colleagues, and teaching graduate counselors-in-training, I've developed an instructional strategy that presents Freud in a clinically relevant fashion. I think students are open to exploring his relevance, even if they have had less-than-ideal past instruction in this regard. And it has also been my experience that when I talk with professional colleagues, those who are "in the trenches" seeing clients every day, many are enthusiastic about reassessing Freud in terms of contemporary clinical significance. Regardless of theoretical orientation, many are open to the idea that Freud remains relevant, though perhaps not in the ways that have been traditionally articulated. Moreover, an assessment of Freud's relevance is an ongoing question of practice. Clinicians-in-training and clinicians can and should evaluate Freud's ideas in light of their experiences in their clinical training and in their subsequent careers, asking themselves: Does Freud still matter, from a contemporary clinical perspective?

Inauguration: To Mark the Beginning of a New Period, Style, or Activity

To do so most effectively, they may need to be offered some assistance in how to structure an understanding of his life and work. I suggest that we think of Freud as someone who inaugurated important therapeutic concerns that continue to have clinical utility. I use the term *inaugurate* carefully; in using this term, I am more interested in these two definitions of the word—"to put something into use or action officially" and "to mark the beginning of a new period, style or activity"; I am thinking less of this definition of the word, "to put someone into an official position with a ceremony" (Walter, 2008).

In other words, I'm not interested in crowning Freud the first King of Counseling; I am interested in describing how he marked a new style, a new way of doing, a new systematizing of practices. It is important to keep in mind that Freud, while he did have flashes of originality and new insight, generally did not come up with totally new ideas or come up with radically different theories and therapeutic interventions. As Ellenberger (1970) says in his comprehensive work on the origins of dynamic psychotherapy, "much of what is credited to Freud was diffuse current lore, and his role was to crystallize these ideas and give them an original shape" (p. 548). This is an important point to keep in mind when referring to Freud's ideas. Freud's thinking was sometimes original but more often *synthetic*.

I acknowledge that considerable work has gone into my reconstruction of Freud in order to make him useful for clinicians today. I also acknowledge that I depart at times from opinions that Freud held about his own work, let alone what other critics have said. For example, he said at one point that "the theory of repression is the corner-stone on which the whole structure of psycho-analysis rests" (Freud, 1914/1957, p. 16). I disagree. The cornerstone of psychoanalysis, considered as a clinical undertaking, is the talking cure. While repression is certainly a major theoretical component of psychoanalysis, it takes a backseat to the central importance of the client and the relationship.

Starting With the Two Most Important Common Factors: The Client and the Counseling Relationship

Thus we begin with the two therapeutic concerns that have been shown by contemporary research to have the largest influence on therapeutic change, the client and the therapeutic relationship. It may seem anachronistic (to judge someone or something in the past according to our present knowledge) to present Freud in terms of this contemporary research, which has been termed the *common factors hypothesis*. But as we shall see, these two factors can be understood to be the primary building blocks of psychoanalysis itself, factors that Freud knew to be of utmost importance to the therapeutic enterprise.

Freud clearly understood the power of the therapeutic relationship and spoke about it repeatedly and in terms that asserted its primary importance, as we will see. And Freud concentrated his energy on working with and describing unique individuals in that therapeutic relationship: Dora, the Wolf Man, Schreber, the Rat Man, Little Hans. Some were his metaphorical companions for years; Anna O.—her real name was Bertha Pappenheim—remained of interest all his life, even though he never personally treated her. He knew—though he could seem to forget—that the patient was of primary importance. Freud becomes least useful when he distances himself from his patients, mostly notably when he follows twisting and winding interpretations that stray farther and farther from the patient's experience, until the patient and Freud are seemingly miles apart, shouting at one another.

Freud Versus Freud: What Did He Actually Do?

Freud's interpretive excesses have long been noted by his critics, and they must still be acknowledged (his treatment of Dora, one of his early patients, is particularly noxious). However, they are not of foundational importance to understanding the *utility* of psychoanalysis. In fact, they show Freud's frequent misunderstanding of the results of his own clinical work; his blunders show that he was relatively unsuccessful when he lost focus on the client and most successful when he demonstrated the qualities that outcome researchers have identified over the years as leading to positive therapeutic change, "factors such as therapist credibility, skill, empathic understanding, and affirmation of the patient, along with the ability to engage the patient, to focus on the patient's problems, and to direct the patient's attention to affective experience" (Lambert & Barley, 2001, p. 358). Freud possessed these qualities and often showed them to patients. And his patients, as patients are wont to do, probably didn't really care much about his esoteric interpretations, but instead remembered the small kindnesses and humanity that he displayed. Freud could be empathic, affirming, and engaging; these qualities have been recorded in stories by and about his patients (Doolittle, 1956; Lohser & Newton, 1996; Ruitenbeek, 1973), and these qualities remain essential—primary—in therapeutic treatment.

Quick Clinical Vignette

The Importance of Being Human

The vital importance of empathically understanding and responding to clients was illustrated to me with the case of Teddy. Teddy was a twenty-one-year-old male who struggled with major depression. We met for about a year, discussing the neglect that had characterized his childhood, his struggles with depression, weight, and keeping in good physical shape, and his attempts to find employment.

As is often the case, there was a negative interaction among his issues—his depression, and the medications that he took for it, led to weight gain, which made him further depressed, which led to more weight gain, which caused him to be more sedentary—all of which impacted his employment negatively. His weight gain caused serious knee and joint problems, making it difficult for him to stand for long periods. Since he couldn't stand, many jobs were ruled out. His overall poor health and fitness ruled still more jobs out, and as a consequence of his depression, he tended to have problems with sleep, either sleeping too much (and missing work) or sleeping too little (and falling asleep at work).

Despite all this, Teddy did improve, and at termination was working steadily part-time. He told me that I had helped him. I asked him how. He said that when he told me about a successful job interview, I had literally jumped up and down with excitement. (I recalled the incident—I had rocketed to my feet and yelled with glee.) He said that no one had ever been excited by anything he had ever done—I was the first person to express joy for him. The takeaway? Even Freud, who advocated restraint and objectivity, was human and real with his clients. If a client tells you something that makes you want to jump up and down with joy, you might consider doing it.

THEMES INAUGURATED BY FREUD

- Importance of client
- Importance of therapeutic relationship—transference and countertransference
- The role of unconscious processes
- Repression of important psychic material
- Resistance to uncovering and acknowledging important psychic material
- Interpretation of dreams
- Role of reason and rationality in therapeutic change
- Sexual drive/Sexual motivation
- Childhood determinants of personality
- Multicultural considerations
- Feminism
- Etiology (origin/cause) of mental illness
- Hypnotherapy
- Electrotherapy
- Psychopharmacology (use of psychiatric drugs)
- Diagnostic classification of mental illness
- Child sexual abuse
- The necessity of counselor self-awareness and self-insight
- The ongoing necessity of clinical supervision and collaboration

The Cause(s) of Mental Illness

An important example is the etiology (origins or cause) of mental illness. In the 1880s, scientific theories of the mind were "in essence barely disguised physiological theories" (Gay, 1989a, p. xiii) that held that organic issues such as brain lesions were responsible for abnormal thoughts and behavior. Patients might be summoned to display their bizarre symptoms in amphitheaters before medical students or the interested public, but in the scientific community at that time it generally wasn't thought useful to listen to them and take seriously what they said. The focus was on determining how organic problems such as brain lesions or tumors produced abnormal behavior. Freud instead began to suggest that there were psychological factors that could produce these behaviors, and his entire project was aimed at finding out their underlying root causes.

Yet the debate between the biological versus psychological origins of mental illness was not thus laid to rest. Freud, who himself began his career in scientific, applied research, never fully abandoned his hopes for a biochemical explanation of brain and behavior. Moreover, the method introduced by Freud's contemporary, Jean-Martin Charcot, involving the "systematic clinical correlation of compromised mental functions with anatomical damage to particular areas of the brain . . . has been the central method in neuropsychology for many years" (Turnbull & Solms, 2004, p. 574). Resurgent research interest in this arena was officially recognized when Congress declared the 1990s the "Decade of the Brain," and there has been a roaring return to inquiry into the relationship between brain structure and functioning and mental health and mental illness.

Transference and Countertransference

As another example, transference (feelings of client toward counselor) and countertransference (feelings of counselor for client) continue to be useful because they illuminate otherwise incomprehensible reactions on the part of clients and equally incomprehensible (and sometimes unethical) reactions on the part of counselors. Helping professionals are less likely to be blind-sided if they are well-versed in Freud's views on the therapeutic relationship. There is a story about a counselor who, confronted with the fact that he had sex with a client, was asked, "Didn't you consider the possibility of transference and countertransference?" He replied, "I don't believe in all that Freudian stuff." There may be plenty of "Freudian stuff" that a clinician can safely regard as optional, but the potency of the therapeutic relationship isn't one of them. Freud remains important because of the fact that many of *his* clinical preoccupations remain *our* clinical preoccupations; the questions raised by *his* theory and practice are the questions raised in *our* contemporary clinical practices. His answers are not always our answers (and they may need significant revision to remain useful to us), but many of his questions retain crucial significance for every therapeutic encounter and we ignore them at our—and our clients'—peril.

Further Developments

And as we shall see, psychoanalysis did not end with Freud. There have been a number of crucial developments in the field. There has been an important transition from a classical model that stresses internal, instinctual drives to an interpersonal model, in which our relationships with other people are not incidental to our development, but in fact fundamentally constitute our growth as human beings (Greenberg & Mitchell, 1983). There has also been a growing concern with multiculturalism and how psychoanalysis can be practiced from a diversity competent and multiculturally aware perspective (e.g., Altman, 2010). There has been important work that aims to integrate neuroscientific findings and psychoanalytic theory (Schore, 1994, 2003, 2011). These important new findings—patches that update the basic program, to adopt a computer metaphor—further support the idea shown that psychoanalysis isn't simply of historical interest, but continues to be highly relevant and a useful model for the contemporary clinician.

Not only highly relevant and useful, but supported by empirical research as well. Shedler (2010) reviews the literature and concludes that the evidence shows that psychodynamic (he uses this term interchangeably with psychoanalytic) approaches are just as efficacious (working in clinical trials) and effective (working in more natural settings) as other psychotherapies. He says there have been chronic misconceptions of what constitutes contemporary psychoanalytic practice, as well as a lack of awareness of the research studies that support its effectiveness. In fact, research supports the use of psychodynamic/psychoanalytic approaches and finds that it is just as effective as other approaches; this equivalence should sound familiar, because it points us back in the direction of the common factors hypothesis that states that different psychotherapeutic approaches are equivalent in their treatment outcomes.

Summary

- Freud's life and work remains clinically relevant for counselors and can be most usefully understood from a common factors perspective that emphasizes the importance of the client and the counseling relationship.
- Freud, when he was most successful with his clients, displayed the care and attentiveness that we now know to be essential for positive treatment outcomes.
- Freud serves as an example of the necessity for counselors to gain insight into their own thoughts and behaviors; he serves as an example to avoid through his inability to collaborate with his peers.
- Freud inaugurated key themes that the field returns to, themes such as the cause(s) of mental illness and the status of unconscious processes; these themes fundamentally define the counseling enterprise.
- Important revisions have been made to Freud's theory. The most important ones are a movement toward an interpersonal model, a concern with multicultural practice, and integration of neuroscientific findings, which all are examined in detail in this book.

1

The Talking Cure

The idea that it is legitimate for one person—a counselor or therapist—to help relieve the mental distress of another person—a client or patient—by talking with them about their problems is pretty much taken for granted today, and psychotherapy has been enshrined in Western culture. While there are a few critics who have critiqued the very legitimacy of psychotherapy in the not-too-distant past (e.g., Masson, 1994), the debate about the therapeutic enterprise has largely died down and psychotherapy has become embedded in contemporary culture. It all began with the case—and the active assistance—of one very exceptional woman, the famous Anna O. The case of Bertha Pappenheim (Anna O. was the pseudonym given to Pappenheim) "ranks as the founding case of psychoanalysis" (Gay, 2006, p. 63). Her centrality in the birth of talk therapy, her exceptional character, and her noteworthy life continues to be of great importance to understanding not only the origins of therapeutic work but also its workings today. We review who she was and why she was so important to the development of Freud's ideas, before going on to examine her contemporary importance.

The First Client: Bertha Pappenheim

To begin, we must reemphasize that Pappenheim was never Freud's patient. She was the patient of a senior colleague of Freud's, Josef Breuer. Breuer treated Pappenheim from 1880 to 1882, and discussed the case with Freud. Freud became intensely interested in it, and he and Breuer spoke many times and at length about Pappenheim's treatment. Pappenheim's case, as described by Breuer, was ultimately published in a book, *Studies on Hysteria,* together with cases that Freud described (Breuer & Freud, 1893–1895/1955).

TREATMENT SUMMARY FOR BERTHA PAPPENHEIM

- Josef Breuer, an older colleague of Freud's, treated her from 1880 to 1882.
- She is considered the founding patient of psychoanalysis, even though she wasn't treated by Freud. Freud first learned of the case in November 1882. He is very curious about it and asks Breuer about it constantly. They have many discussions about Pappenheim's case.
- She called her treatment the "talking cure" and sometimes "chimney-sweeping."
- Her case was published, with Breuer and Freud as the authors, in *Studies in Hysteria,* 1893–1895.
- Pappenheim is described as being extremely bright and talented—but it is her less intelligent brother who is sent to University.
- It was her duty to nurse, day and night, her sick father.
- She develops strange symptoms—a severe thirst (with a corresponding inability to drink water); facial tics; hallucinations; coughs.
- Breuer listens to her, spending over a thousand hours with her during the course of treatment, according to some sources. Unsurprisingly, Pappenheim develops a deep attachment to him, including romantic and erotic feelings.
- Breuer terminates treatment abruptly; Pappenheim's condition deteriorates.
- Pappenheim goes to the Bellevue Clinic in Switzerland, a private sanitorium, and underwent more "treatment"—electrotherapy, massage, rest cure, hydrotherapy.
- Pappenheim gradually improves, likely due to her increased sense of agency and her accomplishments in literary and philanthropic endeavors. She goes on to become an influential social worker and advocate for women's rights.
- Debate continues about the relative merits of Breuer's treatment of Pappenheim. From a common factors perspective, Breuer (1) paid attention to Pappenheim, (2), engaged her in a warm and supportive relationship, and (3), activated hope/placebo factors through his encouragement and support.

What could have interested Freud so much about Pappenheim's case that he kept pestering Breuer to talk about it and to write up a case report on it? Freud's letters to his eventual wife, Martha, describe his excitement discussing cases with Breuer, saying that they ate meals together in their shirt sleeves and had "a lengthy medical conversation on moral insanity and nervous diseases and strange case histories" (E. Freud, 1960/1992, p. 41), one of the more strange being Pappenheim's. For to be sure, Pappenheim's case held many interesting, even exotic aspects. Pappenheim began nursing her father (he had tuberculosis) in July of 1880; she was 21. Over the course of caring for him, she began to develop general weakness, anemia, and an aversion to eating; eventually she developed a nervous cough, which brought Breuer into the picture for the first time in late November. She took to her bed in December; at this point, symptoms started to proliferate. She developed squints and facial tics, headaches, paralysis, and periods of dissociation and altered consciousness. Breuer began to explore these symptoms and to develop a rudimentary method of working with them. Freud's (1909–1910/1961) summary in *Five Lectures* (which condenses and simplifies the complex treatment history) shows his view of Pappenheim's difficulties and Breuer's stumbling attempts to help her: Patient becomes confused and enters a trance-like state; patient mutters a few key words; doctor deepens trance-like state and repeats the key words; patient relates daydreams centering around a young girl caring for her sick father; doctor brings patient back to normal state; patient expresses relief and is improved; wash, rinse, and repeat.

Intensive, Ongoing Treatment

Pappenheim and Breuer remained locked in this pattern for nearly two years; by some accounts Breuer spent over 1,000 hours with his young patient, identifying symptoms, working to release the emotion that had been pent up, usually as the result of an upsetting event, and moving on to new symptoms when the old ones had been dealt with. Pappenheim developed symptoms that were of great clinical interest, such as hallucinations—imagining that her fingers were snake heads—and unusual disturbances of language—at times being unable to speak her native German and instead speaking and writing in English, Italian, and French. She developed terrible thirsts, but could not bear to touch a glass of water to her lips, and for stretches of time subsisted on fruit. And, in a truly odd twist, in the second year of her treatment she began to tell Breuer that she was actually living both in the present and exactly one year earlier.

It appeared that that the symptoms that Pappenheim was displaying could be linked to traumatic scenes that she experienced. In the first place, caring for her dying father was the ongoing traumatic backdrop. It is hard for us, in these days of modern, sanitized medicine and skilled nursing care, to imagine what it must have been like to care for a person who suffered from tuberculosis in the 1800s. Anyone who has read classic novels of the period can call to mind scenes in which a tubercular patient coughs up blood into a basin held by a caregiver. These scenes made up Pappenheim's normal day; she held the basin. So it was no wonder that the stories that she repeated when she was "subject to conditions of 'absence,' of confusion, of delirium, and of alteration of her whole personality" (Freud, 1909–1910/1961, p. 5) began with the story of a girl who was caring for her sick father; this was the fundamental and ongoing crisis that she was experiencing on a day-to-day basis.

Delving into her symptoms—the thirst, her facial tics, the vision where her "fingers turned into little snakes with death's heads" (Freud, 1909–1910/1961, p. 11)—seemed to show that they originated in situations in which Pappenheim experienced, but suppressed, significant emotions. The thirst, accompanied by a horror of drinking, appeared to be linked to a scene where she saw the lap-dog of her maidservant drink out of a glass of water, but suppressed her disgust out of politeness. Freud, quoting from *Studies on Hysteria,* the book he coauthored with Breuer, says that when Breuer was able to induce Pappenheim to repeat this story while she was in hypnotic state, she "asked for something to drink, drank a large quantity of water without any difficulty, and awoke from her hypnosis with the glass at her lips; and thereupon the disturbance vanished, never to return" (Freud, 1909–1910/1961, p. 9).

Freud goes on to discuss the implications suggested by Pappenheim's case: it seems to suggest that "our hysterical patients suffer from reminiscences" and that "their symptoms are residues" and "symbols of particular (traumatic) experiences" (Freud, 1909–1910/1961, p. 12). It is like, he says, walking in a city and coming across the statues of kings or memorials to great, tragic events that a people have experienced; these statues and memorials commemorate important and history-shaping events. In a similar way, symptoms such as Pappenheim's seem to serve as reminders of past, tragic events. The difference is that most passersby in a city go about their daily business, walking past the memorials with hardly a backward glance, intent on their day-to-day life; neurotics, by contrast, not only remember these past events, but "they still cling to them emotionally; they cannot get free of the past and for its sake they neglect what is real and immediate" and "this fixation of mental life to pathogenic traumas is one of the most significant and practically important characteristics of neurosis" (Freud, 1909–1910/1961, p. 13).

Furthermore, it would seem that improvement could be brought about by releasing the emotion that had been stirred up, but suppressed, by the initial traumatic event. Her thirst had been caused by a traumatic experience viewing a dog. Her nightmarish visions seemed to originate in the daymare of treating her sick father. However, her odd experience of living both in the present and exactly 1 year in the past made things more difficult. In the beginning of her treatment, she could simply tell Breuer about her daydreams or her hallucinations and she would be cured. As they entered their second year, Pappenheim had to recall, in exact reverse order, each time the symptom had appeared, a kind of super-duper release of emotions with a chronological twist. To return to the tour metaphor, it was as if Pappenheim not only had to show Breuer the monument, but also had to take him back with her on every trip she had made to the monument, until they reached the original time when the monument had been erected.

Catharsis and Hypnotism

Returning to Freud's simplified version for the sake of clarity—Breuer helped Pappenheim recall her symptoms which then brought her relief—we can clearly see the cathartic cure at work, the idea that therapeutic healing can be accessed by reexperiencing and expressing emotion that had been stirred up by a powerful event but suppressed or not fully worked through. Catharsis has a long history in the Western tradition of philosophy and is particularly associated with Aristotle. In Aristotle's view, catharsis is "a beneficial transformation of painful emotions, through the absorbed contemplation of a powerfully moving artwork, into a key component of a satisfyingly unified experience" (Halliwell, 2005, p. 44). As a theory, it has been applied to artistic expression—poetry, music, painting, and tragedy—as well as more recently to therapeutic expressions of feelings. As Ellenberger (1970) relates, catharsis had been employed for some time in the early 1800s by mesmerists who, under the cloak of arcane ideas like subtle fluids and electromagnetic attraction, had actually been discovering how to establish a hypnotic relationship by developing rapport with their patients. Interest in mesmerism waxed and waned during the 1800s, but catharsis had returned as a topic of interest in the 1880s; this was due in part, interestingly enough, to a book written by Jacob Bernays, the uncle of Freud's wife, on Aristotelian catharsis. Thus at the time of Pappenheim's treatment, "catharsis was one of the most discussed subjects among scholars and was the current topic of conversation in Viennese salons" (Ellenberger, 1970, p. 484).

Yet Freud came to be dissatisfied with the hypnotic technique and the cathartic method that seemed to be suggested by Pappenheim's case and Breuer's work with her. He objected for several reasons. The first was a practical one: he could put only a few of his patients into a deeply hypnotic state and found hypnosis to be "a temperamental, and one might almost say, a mystical ally" (Freud, 1909–1910/1961, p. 20). Put simply, he was lousy at it. Now we might respect Freud for his honesty, but this isn't much of a reason in and of itself. There are other, better reasons that he abandoned hypnosis.

The Psychoanalytic Cure

To understand these reasons, we need to briefly consider what Freud eventually proposed putting in place of hypnosis and the cathartic cure. His proposal constitutes the heart of the psychoanalytic cure—what psychoanalysis tries to do and how it tries to accomplish it, and as such is referred to a number of times in the text. Instead of trying to discharge emotion from a past event using a tool such as hypnosis, he proposed to "uncover repressions and replace them by acts of judgment which might result either in accepting or in the condemning of what had formerly been repudiated. I showed my recognition of the new situation by no longer calling my method of investigation and treatment *catharsis* but *psych-analysis*" (Freud, 1925/1959, p. 30).

ONE-SENTENCE SUMMARY OF FREUD'S AIM IN PSYCHOANALYTIC TREATMENT

The aim of psychoanalysis is to bring unconscious material to conscious awareness and to strengthen the Ego so that it can make rational judgments about this material.

Later, we consider in greater detail what he meant by repression, and what might constitute the kinds of things that a person might wish to repudiate, but for now, let us understand Freud's rejection of hypnosis in the following way: hypnosis was difficult to accomplish, and, as he found out, not necessary. More important, putting people into hypnotic states robbed them of conscious, rational awareness of what was troubling them. They might reveal their deepest anxieties and fears while under hypnosis—they might, as it were, show you around the village square of their mind and show you the sights—but when they woke from a hypnotic state, they would have no memory of the tour they had just conducted.

Instead, Freud developed a method of getting at those underlying issues, which was psychoanalysis itself—making available to our conscious awareness those wishes and urges that we might demonstrate while in a hypnotic state such as Pappenheim experienced so that we can make rational judgments about them—to say no to them, to sublimate them (turn these unacceptable wishes and urges into something productive), or to say yes to them and indulge in them (which is the point of the "horse of Schilda" story in *Five Lectures*). Thus in Pappenheim's case, the critique made from a psychoanalytic perspective is that the cathartic cure that Breuer employed did not help her come to rational awareness of the difficulties that were besetting her and was thus unable to help her make better (i.e., conscious and rational) decisions about them.

Listening to Pappenheim With Sympathy and Interest

These are important theoretical developments that we return to in the course of our discussion, but let us return to our focus on Pappenheim's case. Her clinical manifestations were naturally of interest to Freud, yet he had seen these kinds of florid symptoms before. There certainly were intriguing theoretical issues suggested by Breuer and Pappenheim's cathartic cure, but these bore fruit later. What really interested Freud at the time was his insight that something new was going on, and that insight, stated in the simplest of terms, was that *Breuer was listening to Pappenheim*. Instead of the common approach at the time, which was to dismiss anything said by patients that exhibited psychological distress as hysterical nonsense, Breuer "gave her both sympathy and interest, even though, to begin with, he did not know how to help her" (Freud, 1909–1910/1961, p. 7). This sympathy and interest, this "benevolent scrutiny" (p. 7) was striking to Freud and in *Five Lectures* and elsewhere (e.g., *An Autobiographical Study*) he returns to it with a palpable sense of wonder, despite the intervening years.

This point bears emphasizing, because it is easy, in discussing Freud, to become lost in the critiques and countercritiques that attend his ideas and famous cases such as Pappenheim's. These perspectives add richness, but the primary importance of the case of Anna O., both for Freud and for contemporary practice, is that it pointed out a different way of dealing with mental illness, a way that focused on listening to a person in the context of a warm, empathic relationship. Freud was struck by Breuer's report of this exceptional woman, "bubbling over with intellectual vitality" who possessed a "powerful intellect" and "sympathetic kindness" (Breuer & Freud, 1893–1895/1955, p. 21) and by Breuer's obvious care and concern for a "hysterical" woman, a kind of attitude that went against the grain of treatment at the time.

Pappenheim's Contemporary Importance

We haven't just learned about a troubled person in some far-off time and place; we have learned about a person who has the characteristics of clients that one meets today. She had a number of complex psychosocial stressors. She was struggling with unhealthy societal restrictions, just as many—if not all—of the clients we see today struggle with unhealthy societal constraints, unhelpful messages about sex and gender, race and ethnicity, youth and age, spirituality, and so on. Some of these restrictions are blatant and overt: sexism, racism, and other problems that deny people equitable access to resources and that have severe impacts on their psychological functioning.

In my own experience working in community mental health clinics, many of the clients were so dreadfully lacking in basic resources—jobs, money, education—that it could seem at times that the work that I was doing was a mere Band-Aid. Pappenheim came from a wealthy family, but she was denied access to education and career due to her gender; clients who are seen in contemporary clinical practice may have more equal access to these goods regarding gender, but large barriers remain for large segments of our population due to other factors.

Additionally, Pappenheim displayed a complex clinical picture of possible organic illness and possible iatrogenic (treatment-caused) factors. While modern medicine might have been able to rule out issues such as a seizure disorder, it is also quite possible that it might have failed to add much to the conversation. Suffice it to say that were Pappenheim to be seen today, there may not have been any additional insight into how to describe the complex interplay between her biological and psychological statuses.

She also appeared to have a history of poor medication management and possibly inept psychotherapy. De Paula Ramos (2003) forcefully makes the case that many of Pappenheim's symptoms can be explained by the fact that Breuer prescribed morphine and chloral hydrate at high levels; Breuer periodically tried to wean her off these medications but failed and had to continue prescribing them, which created a rollercoaster of withdrawal and toxicity that most probably contributed to her symptoms.

Quick Clinical Vignette

Enough Medications to Choke a Horse

Pappenheim's case reminds me of a client of mine, Grace, who I cared for in the context of a residential treatment program. As the director of the program, I occasionally took over direct care duties when my staff was unavailable, and when I would administer Grace's medications to her, I would feel queasy at the size, variety, and quantity of the pills that she took—some appeared large enough to literally choke a horse. She took the medications for mood and for her persistent florid symptoms of psychosis—as well as medications to combat the significant side effects from her medications, side effects that included tardive dyskinesia, which can manifest as "abnormal twisting and rocking movements of the body and restless...movements of the feet" (Moncrieff, 2013, p. 77). Grace had other serious medical issues, many of which could have been caused by and/or exacerbated by her many medications, issues such as weight gain, high blood pressure, diabetes, and heart disease.

It was, unfortunately, extremely hard to assess whether her medications in fact helped her—when her psychiatrist changed her medications, Grace would appear to improve, but after a week or two, the symptoms would return with a vengeance. Grace was one of the most heroic people I've ever met. Even when she was in the midst of the most severe psychotic episodes, she would pause and ask me how my daughter was doing. When the staff would sit with her and try to get her to draw (an activity that she enjoyed and that seemed to calm her), Grace would ask me if I thought my daughter would like it. Grace died in her early fifties from heart failure; her life was both tragically foreshortened (those diagnosed with schizophrenia die on an average of 15 to 20 years earlier than the general population [Tandon, Nasrallah, & Keshavan, 2009]) as well as marred regarding her quality of life. The takeaway is that, like in Pappenheim's case, psychotropic medications continue to be potentially helpful and potentially harmful. While mood may be regulated and psychotic symptoms may be dampened, there are significant side effects that can seriously impact a client's quality of life.

Was Pappenheim also the victim of poor counseling? If so, she wasn't the last one to have suffered from this malady. We clinicians hear stories of botched treatment, misguided interventions, and ethical misconduct. One client I saw told me that she had slept with every counselor that she ever had prior to me; I was able to help her break that streak, but the damage that she had sustained from her prior (mis)treatment was appalling. Clinicians, when they are honest with themselves, admit their own treatment blunders (though for most of us, thankfully, they are not such blatant violations of ethical codes). We have been inattentive, said hurtful things without meaning to, and been blindsided by our own biases and prejudices. We have no indications that Breuer acted unethically, but his treatment of her was a haphazard, do-it-yourself kind of affair, and though Pappenheim seemed to get immediate relief from seeing Breuer, the question remains whether his treatment was ultimately therapeutic for her. Pappenheim, with all these variables in play—psychosocial stressors, societal barriers, and biological and treatment questions—was hard to figure out, just like so many of the clients we see in clinical practice.

We learn something essential—the bedrock of psychoanalysis and all subsequent counseling and psychotherapy—in this inquiry into how to help another human being in clinical practice. We must ask, "Who is this person?" and "What is going on with her?" before we can hope to answer, "How can I help her?" What is noteworthy about Pappenheim's case is that many have tried to figure her out. Breuer tried. Freud tried. Many since have tried, albeit vicariously—one edited collection is plainly titled, *Anna O.: Fourteen Contemporary Interpretations* (Rosenbaum & Muroff, 1984), and *Psychoanalytic Approaches for Counselors* is yet another attempt. It is no easy task; we must listen with sympathy and interest and tact, the quality that Freud prized, paying special attention to her admirable qualities of intellect and character even though, to begin with, we do not know how to help her.

Did Breuer Truly "Get" Pappenheim?

Breuer did try to understand Pappenheim's situation, and in many ways he succeeded in his attempt. The problem is that he didn't credit the importance of what he saw with his own eyes. If one closely reads the first two pages of *Studies on Hysteria* (along with the original case history Breuer wrote on Pappenheim's admission to Bellevue in 1882; see Hirschmuller, 1989) one can find evidence that Breuer knew, at least at the level of description, what was "really going on" with Pappenheim, while simultaneously ignoring the importance of what he was seeing. He says, very directly, that this young woman, "bubbling over with intellectual vitality," was denied outlets for this vitality and instead "led an extremely monotonous existence in her puritanically minded family" (Breuer & Freud, 1893–1895/1955, p. 22). She possessed a "powerful intellect which would have been capable of digesting solid mental pabulum and which stood in need of it though without receiving it after she had left school" (p. 21). She had "great poetic and imaginative gifts, which were under the control of a sharp and critical common sense" (p. 21). He says that she is not religious, yet since she is "the daughter of very orthodox, religious Jews, she has been accustomed to carry out all instructions meticulously for her father's sake" and that "in her life, religion serves only as an object of silent struggles and silent opposition" (Hirschmuller, 1989, p. 277). And, critically, he says that

> she embellished her life in a manner which probably influenced her decisively in the direction of her illness, by indulging in systematic day-dreaming, which she described as her "private theatre." While everyone thought she was attending, she was living through fairy tales in her imagination; but she was always on the spot when she was spoken to, so that no one was aware of it. She pursued this activity almost continuously while she was engaged on her household duties, which she discharged unexceptionably. (p. 22)

My reading of Pappenheim's case is that she must have experienced great frustration with Breuer. After all, here was a doctor who took her seriously, who really seemed to understand her situation, who could describe it in such vivid and commonsense terms. He saw that she lived a "very monotonous life, limited entirely to her family" and that she sought "compensation in passionate fondness for her father who spoils her, and by reveling in her highly developed gifts of poetry and fantasy" (Hirschmuller, 1989, p. 277). He saw how smart she was, how passionate, how creative; he also saw how few outlets she had. He saw that she found no solace in the Orthodox Judaism of her father's home, but experienced it as oppressive, which may be unsurprising, as one commentator has pointed out, given the fact that "one of the prayers that Orthodox men chant at their morning prayers thanks God for having created them as men and not women" (Rosenbaum, 1984, pp. 13–14).

And yet this very same doctor, who seemed to understand her so well, most probably did not ask her those questions that would have shown that he was "getting" her, questions like, *So how does it make you feel that you, who are so talented, can't go to university, while your brother can?* Oh, the modern clinician moans, to be able to ask her, *How do you feel about having to live fairy tales in your imagination while you do housework?* To be able to ask, *What do you mean by the words "private theatre"?* To ask, *How does it feel to be on the spot? To know that no one else had been aware that, though you were on the spot, your mind was elsewhere?* It must have been excruciating for Pappenheim—passionate, articulate, and verbal—to lack the opportunity to directly express these feelings.

Empathic Listening and Interpretation

If this sounds traditionally Rogerian rather than traditionally Freudian, it should. A dialectic is often found in counseling programs between Rogers, the empathic listener, and Freud (in this case, Freud/Breuer), the nonempathic interpreter. The idea is that Rogers, the good listener, corrected Freud, the poor listener. Now there is a certain utility in making this generalization, but it is overstated. As we have seen, *the genesis of psychoanalysis emerged not from interpretation, but by listening*. In this earliest phase of prepsychoanalysis, there was little interpretation going on, other than the bare-bones idea of the cathartic cure. Certainly interpretation does appear, in ever-increasing measures, as Freud continues to talk about what happened between Breuer and Pappenheim. Certainly interpretation is a hallmark of Freudian technique, and as such has been vilified as heavy-handed, sexist, clueless, and so on. Certainly Rogers wished to be understood as a kind of anti-Freud. Yet therapy oscillates between listening and interpreting (it can also be seen as the dialectic between acceptance and change, see Linehan, 1993). It is useful for counselors-in-training, who are given a heavy dose of Rogers in courses that teach microcounseling skills, to recognize that Freud, and Breuer before him, listened closely to his patients (the corollary, that Rogers continually interpreted his clients, is a point that cannot be examined at length in this book; suffice it to say that this debate, often happening under the guise of how nondirective a person-centered counselor can be, at the very least admits the use of empathic interpretations [see Kahn, 1999]).

Moreover, it is thus important to note that the prototypical therapy case of Bertha Pappenheim contained both successes in accurate listening—witness Breuer and Freud's eloquent testimony to who Pappenheim was and what she was up against—as well as failures—Breuer's failure to follow up on what Pappenheim was telling him, and Freud's increasing layering of theory that came to obscure the true novelty of the situation. Notably, it contains failures on the part of the clinician to accurately understand data that he himself generated. Breuer's own case notes contain material that he did not follow up on in any practical way; Freud followed this up by neglecting to credit the monumental importance not just of traumatic events, thoughts, and wishes, but of the historical situation that women like Pappenheim were embedded in. This mistake, I believe, continues to be committed with a fair degree of frequency in clinical practice. Sometimes the issue is not a lack of information, it is a surfeit. I have seen clients who had two or three thick binders of treatment history (translation for the modern era: gigabytes rather than the usual kilobytes of data); it was hard to avoid the thought that there had been listening failures, failures that I was at risk of repeating.

The Heroic Client

Duncan and Miller (2000) have described the idea of the "heroic client"; this is not some sentimental notion that we should be nice to clients and say impressive things about them. It is the fact that research supports the very commonsense claim that the single most important thing about the therapeutic encounter is the client. It should come as no surprise that the field of counseling and psychotherapy emerged from listening to a very exceptional person. It is no surprise, but the field has been a long time in coming to that realization. Since Freud, and, some would say, due in part to him, the focus has been on the counselor, on theory, and on technique. Yet Freud is not wholly to blame: even Rogers, in the various iterations of his theory—nondirective, client-centered, person-centered—paid a lot of attention to the ideal attributes of the clinician even as his putative emphasis was on the client. Freud did allow his obsession with theory to overgrow the therapeutic couch, and it can take quite a bit of hacking and pruning to find and set free the person underneath (a florid metaphor, perhaps, but this is after all a text about Freud). In general, the obsession with theory and with the counselor have been constraints that the field has only recently begun to break free from.

Quick Clinical Vignette

The Case of Heroic Helen

After reading about Pappenheim's situation, the reader might feel a little discouraged—how could a woman with so many things going against her find success? Her case reminds me of Helen, who was a client I helped care for in a residential setting. Helen would yell at my staff in person and on the telephone, saying particularly nasty and vicious things. She would appear to ask for help, but then reject it when it was offered. Her moods fluctuated wildly, and she often threatened suicide; there was a safety contract in place, but Helen was masterful at evading attempts to help her.

Since Helen was in Dialectical Behavior Therapy (Linehan, 1993) treatment, which is a skills- and mindfulness-based approach aimed at increasing the regulation of emotions, I worked with staff to refocus their efforts on working with Helen to use her skills in managing her distress—as well as protecting themselves. Helen, who had been repeatedly victimized throughout her life (starting at a young age when she had been sexually offered by her mother to men), was adept at finding and exploiting the softest part of a person's defenses. I continually emphasized to my staff that they should only disclose information that they felt could not be used against them; I modeled this in my interactions with Helen. Helen would ask me about my daughter, and I would tease her and say that she knew that was the one thing I would never talk with her about and she should just give up trying, because I could be just as wonderfully stubborn as she was.

Over the course of 3 years, I became quite frankly pessimistic about Helen's future—it didn't seem that she was getting any more able to commit to her life, much less to enjoy it. She went through some major operations and her health was poor. She was focused on moving to another town and another program within our organization, and I wondered how that would help. I eventually took another position and so ended my involvement with her.

Nonetheless, several years later, I was walking down the street in the town where Helen had wanted to move and heard my name being called. I turned to find an attractively dressed, smiling middle-aged woman looking at me expectantly; I had no clue who it was until she said, "It's me, dummy, Helen!"

I was wonderfully astonished at how great she looked and how happy she acted. She told me that she was enjoying living in town, and we chatted amiably for 10 minutes or so and took our leave of one another with undisguised affection. The takeaway is that, like Bertha Pappenheim and Helen, your clients will frequently amaze you by their heroic transformations despite the great odds stacked against them.

Pappenheim's Amazing Transformation

It took a while for Pappenheim to break free as well. This exceptional woman, who herself came up with one of the best and most pithy descriptions of the therapeutic process, describing it in English as the "talking cure," endured a rocky road to recovery. Breuer ended treatment with her in 1882, and the end of their relationship is subject to conflicting reports. Breuer reports that it was Pappenheim's wish to end it, and that afterward she traveled for a while, and that "it was a considerable time before she regained her mental balance entirely. Since then she has enjoyed complete health" (Breuer & Freud, 1893–1895/1955, p. 41).

We do know from other sources that Pappenheim's struggle to regain complete health lasted for years after her treatment with Breuer, and included stays in the Bellevue sanitorium in Kreuzlingen, Switzerland. A prime difficulty was the aforementioned fact that she was thoroughly addicted to chloral hydrate and morphine and had to be weaned from these drugs, which again has led one modern commentator to diagnose Pappenheim as suffering from dependence on these drugs, with accompanying mood disorders (De Paul Ramos, 2003). She continued to have difficulties; one of the sources we have about Pappenheim comes from Freud's wife, Martha, who kept in contact with Pappenheim throughout the 1880s and into the 1890s. As late as 1887, "Martha wrote to her mother that Bertha was well during the day but still suffered from hallucinatory states in the evening" (Appignanesi & Forrester, 1992, p. 81).

But slowly she improved. She improved so much that her subsequent life is nothing short of astonishing. Pappenheim went on to have an illustrious career as a social reformer and feminist. In 1888, she moved to Frankfurt and engaged in literary activities, publishing a book of short stories in 1890. She began a career in journalism, and she started to reclaim a sense of her Jewish identity. She established the Jewish Women's Union in 1904; in this role, and as a journalist and the founder of a home for at-risk girls and illegitimate children, she crusaded against the sexual and economic exploitation of women (Appignanesi & Forrester, 1992). She became at the end of her life "a deeply religious, strict, and authoritarian person, utterly selfless and devoted to her task, who had retained from her Viennese education a lively sense of humor, a taste for good food, and the love of beauty" (Ellenberger, 1970, p. 481). She died in 1936, and came to be a revered figure, commemorated in 1954 by the West Germany government with a postage stamp that bore her image. If the field of counseling and psychotherapy commissioned medals for Heroic Clients, surely Bertha Pappenheim would have been the first recipient.

Primum Non Nocere—Above All, Do No Harm

It might seem odd to counselors-in-training that we are devoting such space to such a problematic case. Wouldn't it be better to talk about a successful case rather than to one in which therapeutic treatment produced "neither catharsis nor cure" (Ellenberger, 1970, p. 279)? But it is actually entirely correct to do so, both historically and theoretically. Historically, the claim can plausibly be made that Pappenheim's case is not just the founding case of psychoanalysis, it is the founding case of modern counseling and psychotherapy. Simply put, we must study her case because it was the first one that is recognizably a counseling endeavor.

Theoretically, it is important to begin with her case as well. Our field is one in which great harm can be done, and as such we should remember the dictum, *Primum non nocere,* which means First (or Above all) do no harm. *Primum non nocere* has a long if somewhat obscure history (Smith, 2005), and it deserves central billing in any introduction to counseling and psychotherapy. While it must be balanced with other goods such as beneficence, autonomy, fidelity, and justice, and is only one part of a mature model of ethical decision making (Kitchener, 2000), doing no harm, which is termed *nonmaleficence*, is nonetheless a good place to start and to periodically return to. It is difficult to say if Pappenheim's treatment was the cocoon from whence came her colorful career (Appignanesi & Forrester, 1992); what is easier to pick out is that potential and actual harm came from those caregivers who were trying to help her. This is where a book like Masson's (1992) *Against Therapy* come into play, as well as Szasz's (1960) critique of the myth of mental illness, along with other critiques of such professions as social work (Margolin, 1997). They remind us that well-intentioned therapeutic interventions can cause great damage—they *have* caused great damage. It may have become a truism (another bland affirmation, perhaps) to point to the fact that the *DSM* still listed homosexuality as a diagnosable mental illness until 1973 (which it replaced with Sexual Orientation Disturbance [American Psychiatric Association, 1973], see Bayer, 1981), but it is a truism that should be repeated to every counselor-in-training.

Bertha Pappenheim's story deserves its many retellings. It has a happy ending, but that should not make any of us too comfortable or proud. The merit is hers, not Breuer's or Freud's, certainly not commentaries like this one that come so long after the fact. She does us the favor, like all our clients do, of teaching us about what the talking cure does and does not consist of—first and foremost, it consists of listening very closely to a heroic client. This rhetoric—that the client is the teacher who will instruct us, if we are paying attention, how to help them reach their cure—is the best that we know, given the research that we have. A humble attitude—what has been articulated as a position of not-knowing (Anderson & Goolishian, 1992)—is an important way of minimizing harm while attempting to help people.

"The True Vehicle of Therapeutic Influence"

In the first season of the HBO series *In Treatment*, we are shown the relationship between the psychotherapist Paul Weston and his patient, Laura. Paul has been seeing Laura for around a year when the action begins; in the first episode Laura makes a confession: she is in love with Paul. To be more direct: she is in love with Paul and wants to have sex with him. Paul expresses surprise and then lays down the law: the boundaries are clear and ethically prescribed. He is not an option for her. But despite his clear message, things get a bit messy as treatment progresses.

In Treatment is more than just good television. Though it possesses drawbacks, it nonetheless is a big improvement over many other television and movie portrayals of psychotherapy. Paul Weston knows that the "true vehicle of therapeutic influence" (Freud, 1909–1910/1961, p. 57) is the transferential relationship between counselor and client. Transference—"a degree of affectionate feeling (mingled, often enough, with hostility)" (p. 56) that the client feels toward the counselor—reenacts that client's past relationship history. When Laura falls in love with Paul, Paul suggests that the intimacy of the therapeutic encounter stimulates powerful emotions, and that as a result of this, she is transferring feelings from past relationships into the therapeutic relationship with him.

Quick Clinical Vignette

Sometimes, a Brother Is Just a Brother

In considering transference and countertransference, one must be aware that in the treatment encounter there is typically a complex mixture of relatively more accurate and reality-based responses versus relatively less accurate and less reality-based responses on the part of both client and counselor. As an example, I was referred a client whose presenting issue was a series of sexual encounters with married men. As a heterosexual, married male, I carefully prepared myself for our first session. I spoke with my supervisor about the possibility that the client might choose to act seductively with me; I also spoke with my supervisor about how I might caringly and ethically respond, should the client do so.

Susie turned out to be a strikingly attractive, intelligent, and funny woman. She was married to Jeffrey (who was aware that she was in treatment with me and who was unstinting in his support of Susie), had two small children, and was open and articulate in describing her situation. She thought that her status as a sexual abuse survivor played a part in both her problems with alcohol and with her sexual encounters. At the end of the session, she paused and said, "You know, you remind me of my brother."

I was uncertain how to interpret her remark; given the circumstances, I brought up Susie's remark in supervision, and we agreed that I should remain open yet vigilant.

Several sessions passed, and Susie remained the same—funny, kind (to everyone except herself), and engaging. Then, after a few months, Susie greeted me in the waiting room with, "Hey, I want you to meet my brother. Don't you guys look alike?"

Her brother and I could've been twins. Walking with Susie back to my office, we marveled at the resemblance.

Susie's treatment continued to progress extremely well; in fact, her progress was close to ideal—slow, steady, and enduring. Her drinking decreased, her self-esteem improved, and she stopped having sexual encounters outside her marriage.

So what about her remark? I came to believe that it was primarily a statement of fact—we did look very much alike. Seeing me, she immediately thought of her brother.

But I also think that her statement meant something more. We usually think that it is the counselor who needs to manage unruly feelings in session. Yet I believe that Susie was the one who made her treatment more effective by telling herself and telling me that our relationship was going to be intimate but fraternal. In effect, she set the bounds for the treatment alliance, making it as powerful and helpful as a relationship between brother and sister can be—but also clearly articulating the normative boundaries for this relationship. The takeaway? Susie's case furnished an important reminder that, in considering the real and imagined process and content of the therapeutic relationship, look to the client's lead.

As we have already seen in our discussion of Bertha Pappenheim and her treatment provider, Josef Breuer, powerful feelings arose in the first therapeutic relationship. Just how powerfully they were manifested is illustrated in what happened at the end of treatment. We know that Breuer spent an enormous amount of time with Pappenheim; we know that even when she was most downhearted, she took pleasure in his company. We also know that the ending of their relationship was very hard on Pappenheim and that the termination was very poorly executed (Breuer abruptly referred her and then fled on vacation with his wife). We know that throughout the treatment, both Pappenheim and Breuer acted in ways that suggested that there were other qualities to their relationship than those assumed to be typical between a doctor and a patient. It's likely that Pappenheim had fallen in love with Breuer—transference—and it is equally likely that Breuer entertained feelings toward Pappenheim as well—countertransference—even if he never overtly acted on their feelings. In their relationship we see a great example of everything that Freud said about these mutually occurring phenomena. Unfortunately, therapeutic use was not made of these feelings, and we find yet more cautionary evidence from the first psychoanalytic case that should make us yet more careful in our clinical practice.

The Therapeutic Relationship: What's It Really Like?

A skeptic might break in and say, You have shown erotic elements in (1) a television show about psychotherapy and (2) in the first official psychoanalytic case. Surely these elements aren't as important in modern clinical practice? And even if they occasionally exist, why focus on these extreme manifestations of erotic attraction? Isn't the therapeutic relationship more characterized by less extreme characteristics, like warmth, friendliness, and liking (on the positive end) and mild irritation, impatience, and dislike (on the negative end)?

In my experience, and I believe in the experience of most practitioners, it is true that therapeutic relationships are generally much less intense than either Paul's relationship with Laura, or Breuer's relationship with Pappenheim. I have genuinely liked, esteemed, and respected my clients (on the positive end) and occasionally disliked, wondered about, and been irritated by my clients (on the negative end). A few provoked stronger negative feelings; a few caused stronger positive feelings, and the solutions to these potentially unmanageable feelings were the same: consult with colleagues and address these issues in supervision.

And what have my clients thought and felt about me? My best guess is probably pretty much the same as how I felt about them—the vast majority liked or disliked me in varying measures. I don't remember clients who powerfully disliked—hated—me; they probably just didn't come back to counseling. I do remember a small number of clients who seemed to powerfully like—maybe love—me. A few of my "little patients" (as Paul would say) loved me, I think. And at least one of my big patients was powerfully attracted to me. After being in treatment for several months, she revealed that she was deeply in love with me; I was absolutely blindsided, having had no inkling of her feelings. We worked on this in counseling until I left for another position. After we terminated, this client wrote to me, e-mailed me, and called me. She went so far as to contact my parents and woo my father; one of the ways she did this was to ask him to send her the books he wrote as a sociology professor, the surest way into any academic's heart. (Happily, she also sent a letter to him later, in which she apologized and also let him know that she had just married and was feeling much more integrated and healthy and optimistic.)

I don't think her reaction was all about me. Freud tells of an occasion early in his career when he was still using hypnosis. He hypnotized a woman, and when she woke up she threw her arms around his neck; he says that "I was modest enough not to attribute the event to my own irresistible personal attraction, and I felt that I had now grasped the nature of the mysterious element that was at work behind hypnotism" (Freud, 1925/1959, p. 27).

My own client wasn't attracted to me just because of my own irresistible personal attributes, but rather because of the powerful elements that existed in our work together.

Finding the Sweet Spot

The skeptic is right to point out that in most cases, the therapeutic relationship doesn't go to these kinds of extremes, and in fact, Freud (1940/1964) himself asserted that it generally wasn't ultimately therapeutic for the patient to get caught in extreme feelings of love or hate for the therapist. Fortunately, the therapeutic relationship isn't often characterized by passionate feelings. Instead, things like warmth, and trust, and empathy, attentiveness and positive regard need to be present—a nice, warm, moderate, supportive atmosphere that can withstand apathy, challenge, misunderstanding, and so on, a kind of therapeutic "sweet spot" between extremes.

But we know that it always remains incredibly potent, and we need to always be aware that other feelings—other more passionate feelings—can also arise. And if we do not anticipate this, we might be tempted to flee, like Breuer did, or tempted to act on them, like Paul in *In Treatment* (I won't divulge anything more than that; you'll have to watch the series for yourself). And we know that these kinds of responses are antitherapeutic and potentially very harmful: *Primum non nocere*. While we might prefer to focus on the successes of our profession, it is important from a theoretical perspective to also focus on the cautionary tales, of which Pappenheim's is the first. Despite harm generated by well-meaning helpers, Pappenheim heroically cured herself. Pappenheim's story is where Freud began in his five lectures at Clark University in Worcester, Massachusetts, in 1909, and her story continues to offer modern counseling and psychotherapy essential lessons in this the next millennium.

Summary

- From a common factors perspective, the client is where the action is. Thus we begin our inquiry with the first client, Bertha Pappenheim.
- Pappenheim's treatment was complex. Simplified, her counselor helped her recall her symptoms through his hypnosis of her and her own autohypnosis, which brought her relief. In reality, what was most curative was the relationship they formed.
- This early method—the reexperiencing and expressing of powerful, suppressed emotions—is the cathartic cure.
- Freud rejected catharsis and hypnosis. He agreed that the client must bring repressed material to light, but said that the client must be in a conscious

state, not a hypnotic one, so that the client can make rational judgments about this material. Simply reexperiencing the emotions is not enough; cognitive decisions must be made.

- Pappenheim, who became addicted to psychotropic drugs and who was given much-less-than-optimal treatment, continues to hold contemporary importance. Her case reminds us that we can't assume that because we think we are doing good, we are actually doing good.
- Pappenheim's case also furnishes the first example of our clients' ability to transcend their circumstances; she exemplified the idea of the heroic client.
- The treatment relationship is the primary vehicle for positive therapeutic outcome. It is not just the container for active therapeutic techniques and interventions—it is the single most potent intervention itself and cannot be separated from other therapeutic interventions.
- In considering the treatment relationship, the counselor would do well to find the sweet spot between extremes of apathy and disinterest on one hand and overintense engagement on the other; Goldilocks reminds us that the porridge must be neither too hot nor too cold but just right.

2

Basic Psychoanalytic Concepts

Now that we have established the original context of psychoanalysis and counseling and psychotherapy—heroic proto-client collaborates with well-meaning but at times bumbling proto-counselor to create the talking cure—we can now fill in this context with Freud's clinical concerns: his understanding of how the mind worked, how people and their personalities develop or fail to develop, and how someone who wished to help people in a clinical setting could do so. Recall that from a common factors perspective, what we are now discussing is the way that this particular theory, psychoanalysis, organizes what the counselor and client do together in the context of a helping relationship. Using the metaphor of language, this chapter introduces the vocabulary used by psychoanalysts as they work with their clients to understand the issues they face and to achieve positive change in their lives.

As we have seen, Freud fundamentally viewed mental processes as ordered and regulated—"that the mind, however disheveled it might appear, is governed by firm rules" (Gay, 1989a, p. xvi). While Freud's account of the rules that the mind must obey varies at times from earlier and later formulations (Freud tended to modify many of his views, to the exasperation of his followers and to the vexation of his later explicators, making it difficult at times to coherently summarize his perspective), we can nonetheless reconstruct a reasonably simple description that stays true to Freud's vision of what makes people tick. Let us begin by examining both his structural and topographic models so that we may then make clear his views on the essential conflicts that beset human beings.

How the Mind Works: The Structural Model and the Topographical Model

Structurally, the mind comprises three components—the Ego, the Id, and the Superego (I use the commonly accepted translations, but I ask you to remember that the better translations are the I, the It, and the Super-I; see Bettelheim, 1982). The Id is "a chaos, a cauldron full of seething excitations" (Freud, 1933/1964, p. 73) that "knows no judgments of value: no good and evil, no morality" (p. 74). The Id is like a petulant rock star or an out-of-control movie star in a hotel room—destructive, childish, and ordering room service for everything. It wants satisfaction, and it wants it now. And while we might think of it as something only celebrities have to deal with, Freud insisted that the Id structures every person's experience, not just out-of-control celebrities. While many of us might deny that we possess such amoral urges, this is no good defense. In fact, our denial simply proves that these urges are so unacceptable to us that we must disown them.

Then there is the Ego, which "stands for reason and good sense" (Freud, 1933/1964, p. 76) and can be likened to a rider astride the horse of the untamed Id. The Ego is in general that sense of reasonable decision making that we possess when we feel calm and in control; it's the frugal person who doesn't buy the unnecessary pair of shoes, the sensible one who passes on dessert, the financially responsible one who lives within one's means and doesn't max out one's credit cards. A well-functioning Ego, in Freud's view, offers the best hope for a well-ordered and productive life.

Finally, there is the Superego, which "takes over the power, function and even the methods of the parental agency" (Freud, 1933/1964, p. 62) and broader societal demands. This is the part of the mind that can sound like mom or dad telling us to be good and scolding us when we are bad. It can also be more subtle internalized messages from society—messages that tell us what men and women should act like, messages stimulating our desires for sex, money, food, power but also prohibiting and restricting them as well (for example, five commercials that feature fatty and unhealthy food, followed by a show like *The Biggest Loser* that focuses on weight loss). Crucially, the Superego tends to be negative, punishing, and nagging.

The Topographical View

Moreover, these structural elements can be mapped onto a "topographic" view of mental processes. The topographical view was Freud's earlier understanding of the mind and how it worked (which was partially superseded by the later "structural" theory of mind); in the topographical view, there were three mental processes—the conscious, the preconscious, and the unconscious. Freud (1923/1961) describes the conscious as "the surface of the mental apparatus" (p. 19). States of consciousness tend to be transitory, with ideas and perceptions moving into and out of awareness. Consciousness itself is a bit of a slippery term; when Freud discusses it, he can seem a bit defensive and eager to get on to discussing his real interest, the unconscious. For example, at one point he states, "there is no need to discuss what is to be called conscious: it is removed from all doubt" (Freud, 1933/1964, p. 70). He generally appears content to label the conscious as that of which we are aware—"'being conscious' is a purely descriptive term, resting on perception of the most immediate and certain character" (Freud, 1923/1961, pp. 13–14)—and it is a term that we accept in commonsense terms as an identifiable, unquestioned mental process. Though we might struggle to exactly capture what the conscious is, Freud seems to say, we know what we mean when we use that word.

There are two kinds of unconsciousness: "we call the unconscious which is only latent, and thus easily becomes conscious, the 'preconscious' and retain the term 'unconscious' for the other" (Freud, 1933/1964, p. 71). This is an important distinction, because in contemporary usage, we tend to use the word *unconscious* (or that other word that can be a synonym in everyday speech, *subconscious*) for things that we aren't aware of but can be made aware of fairly easily. Thus people speak readily of things existing in their unconscious or subconscious; however, the fact that people are aware of these things suggests that this material is more likely to exist in what Freud is labeling the preconscious. The unconscious is reserved for ideas that resist being brought into awareness, material that resists easy transformation into consciousness. The unconscious, it must be stressed, is not a passive container, but is characterized by "ideas with a certain dynamic character, ideas keeping apart from consciousness in spite of their intensity and activity" (Freud, 1912/1958, p. 262).

The Ego in Conflict

The three structural elements—Ego, Id, and Superego—can be located onto the topographic map. The Id is wholly unconscious and can be repressed or prevented from coming to the surface; the Ego, existing in the conscious, extends down into the unconscious; like the Ego, the Superego bridges between unconsciousness and consciousness.

How do these concepts interrelate? Remember that the Ego's relation to the unconscious Id is like a rider astride a horse—"the horse supplies the locomotive energy, while the rider has the privilege of deciding on the goal and of guiding the powerful animal's movement" (Freud, 1933/1964, p. 77). It is important to underscore the idea that the Id, if properly harnessed, is immensely useful—how much farther and faster can you go on a horse than by foot? How much more work can be done with a horse than by hand? Our very concept of "horsepower" points to our intimate awareness of how useful and potent horses are to humans; in the same way, the Id is immensely useful to the Ego.

But the Ego needs to keep its seat, lest it be thrown and the horse—the animal instincts that know neither good nor evil—go charging off, wreaking havoc as it goes. This isn't easy: the Ego "serves three severe masters...the external world, the super-ego, and the id" (Freud, 1933/1964, p. 77). The demands of these three harsh taskmasters are often in conflict. The Id wants satisfaction—NOW! It doesn't care what others want or whether its actions hurt anyone else; the Id definitely does not play well with others. It throws sand in the face of its playmates, hogs all the toys, and eats the entire birthday cake itself.

The Superego, the internalized father and mother, on the other hand, is problematic in a different way. In internalizing the father and mother, the Superego "seems to have made a one-sided choice and to have picked out only the parents' strictness and severity, their prohibiting and punitive functions, whereas their loving care seems not to have been taken over and maintained" (Freud, 1933/1964, p. 62). The Superego, channeling harsh parental voices, makes exorbitant, unrealistic, punishing demands. The poor Ego is caught between the Id, which is the voice of a screeching, demanding child, and the Superego, which is the voice of the mom or dad scolding, blaming, and nagging.

Regarding the external world, far from always satisfying our deepest narcissistic needs for gratification, it is an enduring source of frustration. From Freud's point of view, society imposes heavy burdens on individuals by requiring them to leave unexpressed their most basic impulses—the sexual and aggressive urges of the Id. He says that "our civilization has been built up at the cost of sexual trends" and that this restriction of sexual instincts "applies equally and perhaps still more to the other ones, the aggressive instincts" (Freud, 1933/1964, p. 110). Freud says that civilization is only possible by suppressing and restricting these sexual and aggressive instincts, but it is important to understand that "the ego does not feel happy in being thus sacrificed to the needs of society" (p. 111).

RELATIONSHIP OF ID, EGO, SUPEREGO, AND EXTERNAL WORLD

- The Id, while powerful and chaotic, is nonetheless essential. We should not eradicate the Id, separate it from the Ego, or deny its existence. The Id is the powerhouse, and even if we could get rid of it (which we can't), we would not have the energy to accomplish life's tasks. Like fire, it can be immensely destructive, but also like fire, it can be used for many different constructive tasks.
- The Ego should be in charge—Freud likens it to a rider on horseback, and in another more modern metaphor, to the driver of a car. The Ego needs to be the one who steers our life, who accelerates when the coast is clear and puts on the brakes when danger is sensed. It is the one who must productively engage the Id, the Superego, and the external world and try to address their competing demands.
- The Superego is the internalized mother and father, as well as societal prohibitions and messages. Negative and punishing in tone, it generally doesn't help us recognize when we are doing something right, but gives attention to our negative thoughts and behaviors—which tends to reinforce these behaviors.
- The external world is, in Freud's view, indifferent at best and uncaring and threatening at worst. Other people are motivated by the same self-focused desires as we are, and society is a compact formed to keep the worst of these desires roughly in check.

Thus the central task of the Ego is to harmonize fundamentally conflicting voices—voices that say contradictory things: *I want special treatment!* and *You may not have special treatment!* and *What would it be like if everybody demanded special treatment?!* Freud (1933/1964) summarizes this conflict by saying that "the ego, driven by the id, confined by the super-ego, repulsed by reality, struggles to master its economic task of bringing about the harmony among the forces and influences working in and upon it; and we can understand how it is that so often we cannot suppress a cry: 'life is not easy!' If the ego is obliged to admit its weakness, it breaks out in anxiety—realistic anxiety regarding the external world, moral anxiety regarding the super-ego and neurotic anxiety regarding the strength of the passion in the id" (p. 78). This is a wonderful summary of the kinds of anxiety that we can feel—we can feel anxious about what is really out there that threatens us, we can feel anxious regarding things we somehow feel we *should* feel anxious about, and we can feel anxious regarding thoughts and behaviors bubbling up from within that we can't seem to control.

Moreover, these operations occur on a mental topography that contains much unconscious territory. This is one of Freud's most original contributions—not that we have an unconscious, but that, again to use the topographic metaphor, it is the very ground on which much mental life stands. Yes, conscious processes do make up some of it—there is a certain amount of cultivated land in this landscape. But much of it is wilderness, and we can't avoid traveling through it every day. We can no more evade the impact of our unconscious desires and wishes than we can avoid standing on the ground. To elaborate on the metaphor just a little further, some terrain—that which is conscious—appears to us to be relatively stable, while other terrain—the unconscious—seems to be itself in turmoil, erupting in geysers or volcanoes, shifting and quaking, appearing solid but in reality a bog. One of Freud's admirable qualities is his realism, and here he seems to be entirely realistic and reasonable in his assessment that it's often the case that "Life's a bitch," to reference the vernacular.

The Ego, astride its fiery steed, the Id, gallops through a landscape that can be serene but is more likely to be treacherous. As the rider navigates the terrain, he or she tries to make wise, rational decisions; unfortunately, the internalized mother/father, the Superego, which should be a source of wisdom and guidance, generally just tells the poor Ego what it is doing wrong and punishes it for its mistakes rather than pointing out what it is doing right and praising it for its successes. And as we recall, the external world demands the sacrifice of sexual and aggressive urges that furnish the Ego with its energy. The Ego is fully potent only with the horse-like Id between its legs, but it is riding in a landscape with signs that say in huge letters, NO HORSEBACK RIDING! It is no wonder that the Ego feels anxious on this exhilarating yet terrifying ride through life.

Freud often expresses things that would make sense to the average person walking through the door seeking treatment, and this appears to be the case here. If you would ask the average client whether they feel sometimes like they are being driven by internal forces that they can't quite name (i.e., which are unconscious), are struggling with self-judgment and self-criticism, are having trouble reconciling their needs for satisfaction with a world that seems hell-bent on denying it to them, and are finding it hard to get a handle on all the conflicting pressures in their life and make them work together rather than at cross-purposes, I believe you would tend to get a great deal of agreement. For instance, it isn't easy for women to harmonize the many competing demands placed on them. There are the internalized self-critiques of one's behavior and looks that may have originated from one's parents (e.g., "Be a nice girl!"). There are societal expectations that can be wildly contradictory and physically harmful (e.g., "Be thin to the point of emaciation—but also be voluptuous and sexy."). And there are the normal sexual and aggressive desires that all humans have but that women are socialized into fearing, denying, and/or rejecting. Life truly is not easy, squeaks the poor Ego.

How People—and Problems—Develop

There is a history to every individual Ego's struggle to bring these divergent forces into harmony—the developmental context for people and their personalities. The struggle that is described above doesn't suddenly start on your eighteenth birthday when you become an adult; the battle begins at birth and becomes all-out warfare in early childhood.

As we've seen from the above structural/topographic discussion, Freud believed that conflict was inevitable; it was built into the very essence of what it is to be human. From birth, the infant is driven by wants and needs that demand satisfaction; from the very first time that these desires are frustrated, it knows conflict and anxiety. Adopting a commonsense perspective, we can understand that much of infancy and early childhood consists of the soothing satisfaction of basic needs—sucking at the breast, having one's needs for social stimulation met—and irritating, and perhaps even enraging, denial of these needs—the caregiver who doesn't come to the crib in the night at once or at all, the breast or bottle that is withheld, the failure to give social interaction when the infant wants and needs it.

The child is, in Freud's (1926/2002) words, a "pathetic, helpless thing in the face of an over-powerful outside world full of destructive effects" (p. 112) and the equally scary inner world of the Id, which is present in a person from birth. We can perhaps more readily understand how the outside world is traumatic—it is filled with loud noises, with surprising and scary scenes, with incomprehensible surprises. There are obvious macro-traumas like accidents, abuse, and neglect. But even when infants are relatively well cared for, it can be traumatic to the infant to realize that its basic desires will not always be satisfied; sometimes its cries for food and care will be disregarded, or even when the care is offered, it is not synchronous with its requests. These micro-traumas happen repeatedly, chronically, and repetitively.

To understand how the Ego can regard its own inner world as traumatic requires a little more explanation. Infants appeared to Freud to have been born with a well-developed Id. In fact, this is precisely the point that failed to endear him to his colleagues and the general public: Freud believed that infants are born with powerful and instinctual sexual and aggressive urges. And even more problematically, the infant's Ego is not correspondingly developed: "even for those beings who go on to develop a viable organization of the I, this I is feeble in their childhood years and poorly differentiated from the It" (Freud, 1926/2002, p. 112). Thus the stage is set for the kinds of internal trauma that Freud thought was endemic to early childhood. He asks the reader, "just imagine what happens when this powerless I is confronted with a drive-demand on the part of the It, which the I would like to resist because it senses that the gratifying of this desire is dangerous" (p. 112). The point is that the infant Ego can be scared by its own Id; it confronts not just a scary outer world, but also an inner world that can be even scarier.

What happens, in Freud's view, is that the developing human can begin to regard its own desires and needs as overwhelming; in his terms, the insatiable needs of the Id can overwhelm the resources of the feeble, poorly differentiated Ego. In the best case, the weak Ego develops so that it can ultimately deal with that which is unbearable or distressing by "recognizing it, considering it, making judgement upon it and taking appropriate action about it" (Freud, 1936/1964, p. 246). In the worst case, the Ego cannot withstand these distressing demands and rejects them immediately, and a split develops between the Ego and the Id. This can take the form of denying that the Ego and the Id are a vitally connected team; the Ego can reject not just the Id's demands, but also their intimate relationship. In doing so, the Ego "deals with this danger posed by the drive by treating it as though it were a danger from without" (Freud, 1926/2002, p. 112) and withdraws from the Id. This process is repression.

Repression

In Freud's view, repression can lead to disaster. The Ego and Id are necessarily, intimately related; the Id provides the vital life energy to the Ego and the Ego harnesses the Id and directs this energy into useful, profitable efforts. To ring the changes on the rider metaphor one more time, the horse serves the rider by providing the horsepower for carriages, herding, and pleasure-riding (as well as, unfortunately, the making of organized warfare); if the horse runs away, the man is left without transportation, a means of sustaining himself—and defenseless. The "synthesis has been disturbed" (Freud, 1926/2002, p. 113) and "the repressed impulse is now isolated, left to its own devices, inaccessible but also beyond influencing" (p. 113) while the Ego wanders around on foot.

But things don't stop there. There could be an undeniable relief for the Ego to be separated from the wild demands of the Id—for a time. At first, the Ego may perceive that life is quieter and more orderly through pushing away these instinctual demands. But while there may be momentary success in repressing the unwanted drive-demand, the Id and its instinctual demands and drives retains their potency and power, but now they "have broken away to pursue their own ends without consideration for the interests of the whole person, from now on obeying only the laws of primitive psychology that rule in the depths of the It" (Freud, 1926/2002, p. 113). Simply repressing them does no good—like a game of Whack-a-mole, the drives pop up elsewhere. As Freud describes it in *Five Lectures,* the result of repressing desires will often be failure, and "*the repressed wishful impulse continues to exist in the unconscious*" (Freud, 1910–1911/1961, p. 26). He likens repression to a lecture hall, wherein there is someone in the audience who is so loud and obnoxious that no one can pay attention to the lecture. The lecturer stops and announces that he can't go on and enlists a number of people to put the interrupter outside the hall so that he can continue his lecture. However, the troublemaker refuses to go away, and continues to shout and bang on the door. Putting chairs under the door handles to prevent the troublemaker from reentering the hall (which is the metaphorical equivalent of resistance, the efforts to keep repressed material in the unconscious) doesn't help at all; the troublemaker may not be able to get in, but the ruckus that he causes continues to make the audience uncomfortable, and the lecture turns out to be a dismal failure.

This is, in Freud's (1926/2002) view, the "simple formula for the origins of a neurosis: the I has attempted in an inappropriate fashion to suppress certain parts of the It; this attempt has failed and the It has taken its revenge" (p. 113). Note the word "inappropriate." It is inappropriate to flee from the demands from the Id just as it is inappropriate to attempt to resist it with force. The Id is powerful and must be dealt with in the same manner as you would try to ride a barely tamed horse or quiet an unruly, possibly drunk or unhinged audience member: very carefully. In Freudian terms, human development occurs through nuanced negotiations with the life forces that propel people through childhood and into adulthood; problems develop when these negotiations break down and the Ego treats its own drives as something foreign and tries to flee or fight, both of which tend to be inappropriate and ineffective options.

THE DEVELOPMENT OF NEUROSES

There are three variables that may lead to the development of neuroses. The interaction among these factors can provoke damage.

1. If the child's Ego is particularly weak, then even normal, small, upsetting events could provoke lasting damage.
2. If the child is exposed to external trauma including inattentive parenting at the less extreme, neglectful parenting at the more extreme, and actual physical and sexual abuse at the most extreme, lasting damage can result.
3. If the child's Id is particularly strong, then the child may be damaged by internally experienced trauma.

(Continued)

(Continued)

Freud's thinking is an early form of the vulnerability (or diathesis)-stress model, which continues to be an important theoretical way to understand the development of psychopathology (Hankin & Abela, 2005).

- In this model, vulnerability in a person (be it biological, cognitive, social, or other) interacts with environmental stressors.
- People vary in their predisposition to developing illness; for those with high tolerance for stress/less predisposition to develop a particular illness, it would take a lot of stress to trigger that illness. For those with a low tolerance for stress/greater predisposition to develop a particular illness, it would take less stress to trigger it.
- Freud says that we vary in how strong our Ego is (i.e., in how predisposed we are to develop neurosis) and says that stress can be externally generated by the scary world outside of us, or internally generated by the scary world inside of us.

Freud's Mechanisms of Defense

This is the context for understanding Freud's famous defense mechanisms. Freud (1937/1964) said that defense mechanisms "serve the purpose of keeping off dangers" (p. 237). He acknowledged that they do accomplish this task to a certain degree and that "it is doubtful whether the ego could do without them altogether during its development" (p. 237). The key thing to keep in mind is that they are used within the context we have described above, in the struggle of the Ego to balance and manage the competing desires of Id, Superego, and the external world and the anxieties that result from these conflicts. Freud (1937/1964) claims that "no one individual, or course, makes use of all the possible mechanisms of defence. Each person uses no more than a selection of them" (p. 237). Overall, Freud says that defense mechanisms are useful to a certain degree, are needed in our development, that individuals tend to prefer certain ones and not use them all, and that they will provide the astute clinician with ample evidence of their defensive style. The idea is that the clinician will be able to recognize defenses because they will seem like out-of-place, unnecessary, and ill-fitting responses to circumstances and situations—either in the treatment setting itself or in the client's presentation of external or internal conflicts. Their responses will seem like knee-jerk, inappropriate reactions. One modern commentator thus defines a defense mechanism as "an unconscious subjective distortion that reduces intolerable affect and conflict through automatic and undifferentiated responses" (Clark, 1998, p. 12).

Repression, Revisited

An important point to remember is that some strategies are relatively more dysfunctional, some are relatively neutral, and others are relatively functional; the range has also been described as varying from relatively narcissistic, immature, and neurotic strategies to relatively mature and functional strategies (Vaillant, 1977). Repression is a primary defensive mechanism. It is unavoidable. It is in many ways the substratum of the other defense mechanisms—as Freud (1937/1964) says, the various defense mechanisms are subtle or not subtle repressive methods that the Ego uses and that falsifies its perception of the Id and thus gets only a distorted vision of its own fundamental functioning. No Ego can fully see and accept the Id; it is too painful to contemplate, and repression is the inevitable result. But while it is unavoidable and fundamental, repression is also the most purely dysfunctional defense mechanism. Repression is a turning away from one's very nature, yet "one cannot flee from oneself; flight is no help against internal dangers" (Freud, 1937/1964, p. 237). Repression—trying to flee from oneself—is ubiquitous, unavoidable, and deeply dysfunctional.

Denial

As we consider other defense mechanisms that are generally of dubious value, we need to bear in mind that they were employed for a reason. Attempting to suddenly replace longstanding defense mechanisms may be ill-advised, and clinical work in addressing these mechanisms should be cautious and careful. For example, denial appears to have little useful value; it's hard to understand how consciously refusing to accept reality has any enduring adaptive utility. But like repression, denial is a very common strategy employed by human beings, and clients we see may be able to function on a day-to-day basis only through the denial of unpleasant realities. It is the clinical task to note denial but not necessarily address it directly, unless and until more functional strategies emerge that might replace it, and the same goes for the rest of the defense mechanisms.

Displacement and Projection

Displacement, in which one shifts reactions from one person or situation to another person or situation, is another mechanism that appears to be relatively harmful; displacement tends to add more problems to the original problem (for example, if you displace your anger against a parent onto a spouse, you have not solved the original problem of your relationship with your parent, but you have now created another problem with your spouse). Projection, in which you attribute your own thoughts and feelings onto others, is another mechanism that tends to produce more problems than it solves; it creates a false and confusing world in which you cannot accurately identify who feels and thinks what.

Reaction Formation, Rationalization/Intellectualization, Introjection, Identification, Regression

Other mechanisms can be seen as potentially useful at certain times and in certain ways. Reaction formation occurs when you deal with unacceptable urges and anxieties by expressing the opposite of these urges; if you feel hurt or rejected by your partner, you might conceal your feelings of anger and instead act with renewed kindness and care. This might be an adaptive thing to do, since it might help preserve an important relationship. In rationalization and intellectualization, you attempt to rationally explain away your disappointments; since, as Freud suggests, life is often disappointing, it might be a good thing to be able to soften the heartache we feel when things don't go well for us, as they often don't. Introjection, in which one takes in the values of others, and identification, in which one identifies with the characteristics of others, can also be seen as relatively useful in certain situations. Regression, in which you might return to an earlier stage of development, is an interesting case; it appears to be a relatively common mechanism for children to employ and may be seen as reflecting normal childhood development, but if employed as an adult, it would appear to be a less useful and infantile reaction.

Sublimation

Finally, sublimation is the one defense mechanism that Freud tends to hold up as our best option. He says that sublimation, "in which the energy of the infantile wishful impulses is not cut off but remains ready for use," is indeed a great achievement and that "it is probably that we owe our highest cultural successes to the contributions of energy" (Freud, 1909–1910/1961, p. 60) that can be harnessed through sublimation. It is the closest we can get to turning the light and heat of the Id into pure creative and useful energy for ourselves and broader society and his daughter, Anna Freud (1936/1993), suggested that "it pertains rather to the study of the normal than to that of neurosis" (p. 44). (It is interesting that Freud's daughter wrote extensively about defense mechanisms; could that have anything to do with how she felt about her father?) Clark (1998) reviews research on the topic and states that "the status of sublimation as a defense is questionable because of its unique function of pursuing creative activity in response to threat, presenting more of a coping, rather than a defensive, process" (p. 7).

Don't Forget: Sex Can Be Fun!

But Freud does caution us that even sublimation can be overused. We must not forget that some satisfaction of our (sexual) urges is healthy and necessary; the horse must be fed oats or it will die. As he famously said, "sexual love is undoubtedly one of the chief things in life, and the union of mental and bodily satisfaction in the enjoyment of love is one of its culminating peaks. Apart from a few queer fanatics, all the world knows this and conducts its life accordingly" (Freud, 1915/1958, pp. 169–170). In plain words, don't sublimate all your sexual urges—have sex sometimes too! It is a truism but important to remember that Freud practiced in a time when, at least in the middle and upper classes, sex was mired in repressive gender and economic politics that limited both male and female sexual expression and sadly hindered a full and rich enjoyment of it; it is also important to remember that, while today we may appear to be sexually liberated, in fact many people continue to find difficulty in finding enjoyment in one of life's culminating experiences. Perhaps it is just as useful today as it was in Freud's time to remind clients, and ourselves, that sex can actually be fun.

Quick Clinical Vignettes

Defense Mechanisms in Action

Clark (1998) suggests that there is a "lack of consensus on a universally accepted list of defenses" (p. 8); the following vignettes illustrate some of the more commonly discussed ones. Additionally, he suggests that we should also keep in mind that contextual developmental factors such as chronological age, gender, culture, and family affect a person's use of defense strategies.

Denial—I did an initial intake with a man who said that his ex-wife was threatening to haul him into court to take away his rights to see his kids because she said he drank too much; he was seeing me in hopes I could vouch for him to the judge that he didn't have a drinking problem. This man was sitting two feet away from me, wearing a Miller Lite cap and a Budweiser T-shirt; I also detected a pretty strong smell of alcohol on his breath. His was a living, breathing example of denial.

(Continued)

(Continued)

Displacement—I counseled two children who had been referred to treatment by child protective services; their mother, who was still smarting from what she perceived as hostile and condescending treatment from child protection, treated me with sarcasm and ridicule—"why are you asking me what's wrong with my kids, that's what you get the big bucks for, Mr. PhD!" She displaced her feelings of anger against the protective services worker (who was quite firm and even tough in her approach) onto me (I was soft-spoken and empathic).

Identification—I counseled a boy who once told me, "I'm a Thibodeaux; we all end up in jail eventually." While he could see that he needed to change if he was to avoid this fate, he frequently stated that it wasn't much use to try, because being a Thibodeaux meant that being bad just came naturally. His identification with his family was so powerful that he just couldn't seem to entertain any other way of being in the world.

Intellectualization—A client, whenever he got close to discussing emotional topics such as the death of his wife (which precipitated a severe depression and caused him to seek counseling), brought up philosophical traditions such as Stoicism. When I asked about his feelings about the death of his wife, I was met with rather arid, empty intellectual "philosophizing" that tended to bore and irritate me and challenged me to be empathic with him.

Reaction formation—In a session of couple counseling, a man expressed his suspicion that his wife has had a number of sexual affairs. His wife denied it and expressed heartfelt, if somewhat puritanical and rigid, religious beliefs; however, she also made a number of sexually suggestive comments, dressed in a very low-cut blouse, and acted in a way that I found sexually suggestive. In this case, the woman may have formed excessively moralistic and puritanical beliefs in response to sexual urges that she rejected overtly but displayed covertly.

Projection—The above example also serves as an example of projection. In the session, the woman accused her husband of being the one who wants to have affairs, saying that he wanted to do all sorts of disgusting sexual things. Her husband denied this, saying that she is the one interested in doing them. When I enquired into these practices, the woman in turn projected her own concerns with sexuality onto me, saying that this proved that I was just like her husband and every other man—all men are sexually obsessed.

Sublimation—Once I counseled an eleven-year-old boy who had been referred to our clinic for a variety of serious acting-out behaviors at school, including sexually explicit remarks to one girl and grisly violent threats to another. He was a small boy who appeared much younger than his age and had been bullied at school.

As soon as I opened the door to my office, he rushed in and started knocking things over. His mother rushed around, trying to get him to stop; after a few seconds, I went over to my wastebasket and kicked it. It made a big "bang!" and the boy and his mother stopped and looked at me, thunderstruck. I picked up the wastebasket and turned it over and began to drum on it; after a couple of seconds I smiled at the boy and he came over and we drummed together. As we made rhythmical noises, it came to me—I had read in his report that one thing that he enjoyed was music. The boy and I spent subsequent sessions making musical instruments together—it felt like we were finding ways to modify extreme sounds (the hateful speech that he directed toward the girls) into something that could be listened to with pleasure.

Regression—I counseled a fourteen-year-old boy who wore all black and listened to death metal music. Yet when he was upset, he would pull out a pink binky and stick it in his mouth. Amazingly, he managed to do this behavior without being teased at the alternative school he attended; he had a quick wit, and if you teased him, thinking that you had an easy target—a big baby—on your hands, he would let fly with a zinger. (Removing a pink binky and delivering a zinger that silences your opponent must be its own category of defense mechanism.)

Repression—In working with one client with schizophrenia in a residential, my staff and I noted that she only spoke of a deeply traumatic event that she had witnessed—her father had shot himself in front of her and her siblings—when she had decompensated to the point of needing to be hospitalized. There would be hints in the days and weeks leading up—hints that contained references to trucks and tires and sidewalks (her father had driven cement trucks). When she became intensely psychotic, her speech conveyed a child's primal terror at witnessing such an event. To use a construction metaphor, it was as if this experience had been covered in a layer of concrete; however, it was also as if this layer of concrete had been poured over a volcano, which would periodically vaporize the protective layer of cement and erupt.

The Therapeutic Aim of Psychoanalysis

Let us turn to the therapeutic task, described psychoanalytically. Since Freud is often his own best explicator, we will introduce a lengthy quote that lays out his treatment prescription:

> Our therapeutic aim is easy to outline. We want to restore the I, release it from its limitations, and give it back the dominance over the It that it lost as the result of its early repressions. This is the sole point of analysis; our whole technique is directed to this end. We must locate the repressions that have occurred and induce the I to correct them with our help, to find a better way of dealing with conflict than flight. Since these repressions are rooted in early childhood, our analytical work takes us back to that period as well. It is the symptoms, dreams and free ideas of the sufferer that point the way towards the mostly forgotten conflict situations that we want to bring back to life in the patient's memory. Of course we first have to interpret and translate these indicators, for under the influence of the psychology of the It they have taken on what we perceive as strange forms of expression. On the basis of the ideas, thoughts and memories that the patient is able to pass on to us, not without an inner struggle, we can assume that they are connected with what is being repressed or are derivatives of it. By urging the sufferer to overcome his reluctance to communicate, we educate his I to conquer its tendency to flight and to be capable of bearing the approach of the repressed. Ultimately, if we have

succeeded in re-creating the circumstances of the repression in his memory, his compliance is splendidly rewarded. The effects of the lapse of time work in his favor, and whatever had his childhood I take flight now appears to his grown-up and stronger I to be just child's-play. (Freud, 1926/2002, pp. 114–115)

A SHORT SUMMARY OF PSYCHOANALYTIC TREATMENT

Remember the one-sentence summary of Freudian psychoanalytic treatment: ***The aim of psychoanalysis is to bring unconscious material to conscious awareness, and to strengthen the Ego so that it can make rational judgments about this material.*** Toward that end, accomplish the following:

- Encourage your client to freely produce material. Ask exploratory, invitational questions like "So what's on your mind?" and "What have you been thinking about this week?" and "Tell me more about (your wife, your boss, your feelings about your situation, etc.)."
- Encourage your client to share his or her dreams, daydreams, and reveries.
- Encourage your client to share material that may seem illogical, confusing, or bizarre, including thoughts and behaviors that have been labeled by him or her or others as symptoms, problems, mental illness, and so on.
- Listen attentively and seek to empathically attune yourself to what your client is saying.
- Pay attention to your relationship with your client, especially to times when her or his reaction to you, or your reaction to him or her, seems a bit "off," a bit odd, a bit inexplicable.
- Listen especially closely to patterns of thoughts and/or behaviors that can be traced back to childhood, and inquire into connections that the client might see to present thoughts and behaviors.
- Slowly begin to help the client translate his or her "strange forms of expression"—the totality of the material that has been unearthed in your work together that doesn't make sense, is self-defeating, is illogical, is scary or traumatic, is deeply connected with childhood memories and behaviors, is felt by the client or you to be deeply significant, and so on—into a language that can be understood by your client. Point out connections between past and present thoughts and behaviors, clarify possible patterned responses that the client has in her or his interpersonal relationships, and assist the client in becoming actively aware of her or his mental life, including and especially those thoughts and behaviors that have been unconsciously rejected.
- Acknowledge instances wherein your client's relationship history appears to be repeating itself in your treatment relationship. (You should also be aware when your own relationship history is intruding.) Empathically and tactfully help the client experience new and more satisfying ways of relating to another human being rather than simply recapitulating older relationship patterns.
- Encourage your client to regain control and a sense of agency. Help her or him realize that we are not at the mercy of our childhood experiences, that

what was unbearable or impossible to withstand in the past might now be no more than "just child's-play."

- Encourage a more rational look at our lives and the choices we make. As appropriate, submit to them that we can reject certain choices, accept others, or transform still others.
- Encourage varied, rich, and complex interpersonal strategies, being mindful that overusing even potentially helpful strategies can render them noxious.
- Encourage a tolerant, humane, wise attitude about human nature—that it can contain the most disturbing thoughts and desires, as well as the most altruistic and kind. Anything that a human being has done or thought is, by definition, a human thought or act. These include actions by Hitler and the Dalai Lama.
- Encourage a realistic and Stoic attitude toward life and the satisfaction of hopes and dreams.

As we have seen, difficulties develop when the Ego cannot successfully mediate between the exorbitant demands of the Id, the punishing moralizing of the Superego, and the harsh reality of the external world. In our treatment, we must go back to early childhood, since this was when the weak and underdeveloped Ego began to be overwhelmed in its primary task. By looking at the client's symptoms, examining the client's dreams, and paying attention to the flow of ideas—especially when this flow is disrupted—we can facilitate the process of bringing unconscious material into the client's conscious. This material that we have helped the client unearth will appear strange; remember that the original impulses were likely pretty icky, and the Ego resisted direct examination of these impulses. So they have been disguised, transformed, and changed; the analyst's job is to translate these weird forms of expression back into the original language of sexual and aggressive urges.

Resistance

This process will not be easy, and the analyst must help the client stay in treatment by motivating him or her through an illustration of the benefits of treatment. The analyst should not be surprised if the client displays resistance toward the unearthing of unconscious material or particular suggestions about what this material might mean (or, indeed, the entire treatment process). Resistance can be explained as fear reaction, as the link that the maturing person makes between the now-repressed material and the potential trauma of dealing with it—after all, in the initial situation, didn't the material provoke fear and flight? But in doing so, the maturing person neglects the fact that he or she has developed and that the resources of the Ego have grown and could now perhaps deal with the previously ungovernable reactions. This is where the analyst helps the client rationally address old traumas, putting the Ego back in relation with these rejected parts of itself and restoring the Ego as the benevolent ruler of its passions. The analyst needs to convince the client's Ego that there is a better way than fleeing from the Id—that what seemed so scary in childhood may appear to be nothing more than child's play now. As the saying goes, when you get bucked off a horse, get right back on. The analyst functions as a riding instructor, helping the client conquer his or her fears, and the ultimate result is that the Ego is put back in the saddle.

Progress, Slow and Steady

The point needs to be made that though this quote makes the process sound simple, Freud was clear that treatment is often slow and laborious. Moreover, he believed that this was actually a good thing and that we should be wary of treatment that feels glib and easy. Freud believed that people fall ill from frustration in dealing with life and that symptoms can serve as substitute satisfactions. Symptoms can be seen as a person's unconscious strategy for dealing with an unbearable reality; this is not to make a judgment on their character. As Freud makes clear, we all fall on the continuum of healthy and neurotic behavior and we all manifest thoughts and behavior that could be seen as perverse, neurotic or hysterical (Freud, 1905/1953) and we are all only somewhat normal (Freud, 1937/2002). In the same way, we are all more or less successful in dealing with life, and symptoms can represent relatively dysfunctional ways of dealing with life's challenges.

To review what we have said about defense mechanisms, people often overuse a few strategies to deal with life. But life is much too complex to deal with in this simplistic fashion, and when people fail in the central task of mediating between the many and complex demands in their lives, they can become frustrated and may take flight into illness. In treatment, then, clinicians must be aware that clients will use their preferred interpersonal strategies with them—this is where, again, the idea of transference comes in. It is highly instructive to experience a client and the strategies that they are using to make you like them, make you feel sympathetic, interested, and so on. Their particular constellation of attempts, exactly how they do this with us, is what gives us a sense of their past relationship histories as well as a sense of who they are and what their world is like now.

Freud cautions against falling in with these strategies too quickly; by the very fact that they are unhappy with their lives to some degree, these strategies aren't fully working for them. The analytic treatment—and treatment from any theoretical perspective—needs to offer the opportunity to discover and to practice new methods of getting interpersonal needs met. There will likely be some frustration felt by clients in this process; learning new things can be very difficult—otherwise we would all play the piano like virtuosos. Freud (1919/1955) believed that it was important to avoid quick and easy fixes with clients, because "in so doing they make no attempt to give him more strength for facing life and more capacity for carrying out his actual tasks in it" (p. 164).

Three Choices

In the process of helping clients develop the strength to face life more directly, the analyst also helps the patient decide—what do you want to do with this unearthed unconscious material? As stated previously, Freud (1909–1910/1961) himself pithily offered three possibilities—Say yes to the unearthed desire, say no, or sublimate it—transform it into something productive. Again, there seems to be a great deal of clinical utility in this therapeutic heuristic (quick, rule-of-thumb reasoning), one that can be offered in a humorous fashion to clients—Just say No; Just do it; or be like Mike, as three (somewhat dated) cultural slogans express them. Freud, like his patients, was the product of an age that was synonymous for sexual repression, a culture that tabooed masturbation and other non-harmful forms of sexual expression. For them, there was a great deal of behavior to which society said no; a correspondingly great deal of anguish could be eliminated by rationally and calmly looking at a form of outlawed sexual behavior and saying, Is there any harm in doing it? If not, why not say yes?

And while Freud would've been primarily interested in sexual repression, due to his social and intellectual context and personal sexual history (remember again, we are "doing Freud" when we examine his ideas this way), there is no reason that this can't be applied to other areas of life as well. Certainly anger continues to be tabooed; it can be very therapeutic to unearth anger and to realize that accepting it and feeling it neither makes one a bad person nor necessarily leads to acting on it. Primitive aggressive and sexual feelings—what Yeats (1996) famously described as "Lust and rage" (p. 312)—exist within us all. If we continue to ascribe to the idea that it is useful to acknowledge their existence and in a certain way say yes to them, then we are following one of Freud's three choices.

On the other hand, there are many behaviors that are best rejected. Societies proscribe behaviors such as murder, rape, theft, and embezzlement, as well as a number of less spectacular ones. Through the process of analysis, one might unearth murderous desires; these desires may be related to the primitive rage felt from early childhood trauma. It is important to acknowledge that these feelings are understandable, and that it is not wrong to experience them. But, obviously, the behavior—actually killing someone—is wrong. Moreover, while behaviors may be the largest category of proscribed phenomena, one could argue that certain cognitions—the cognitive distortions that allow a pedophile to prey on children without feeling guilty, for instance—should be rejected as well. And, while it can be therapeutic to fully experience strong emotions, it can be antitherapeutic to stay stuck in them. Forgiveness and the practice of a compassionate non-judgmental attitude are two contemporary mindfulness practices that seek to help people be ultimately released from emotions such as hatred and revenge that prove detrimental to emotional health if held on to.

The third option is sublimation, which we have discussed as the transformation of unacceptable urges into art and other personally and socially useful activities. Freud had high praise for this process, "in which the energy of the infantile wishful impulses is not cut off but remains ready for use" (Freud, 1910–1911/1961, p. 60), saying that "it is probable that we owe our highest cultural successes to the contributions of energy made in this way to our mental functions" (p. 61)—painting, theater, music, architecture, crafts, and professions, all the kinds of productive and satisfying activities that human beings can make and enjoy. As we have seen in our discussion on defense mechanisms, sublimation is the one that comes the closest to a win-win for the individual—while the direct gratification of the primitive desire is not accomplished, there is indirect gratification. And since sublimation tends to lead toward productive activities that are socially sanctioned, the individual can also experience the positive results that tend to accrue from this kind of activity—recognition, prestige, and feelings of pride and accomplishment, not to mention the possibility of career monetary gain.

The Tools of Psychoanalysis: The Background of Freud's Technique

There are several important preliminary points to consider about the development of Freud's technique. First, we recall that Freud's development prefigured important therapeutic themes that the field returns (and returns) to. Remember that it was suggested that Freud inaugurated key counseling concerns; we can see this with crystal clarity in the progression of his technical work from catharsis and hypnotism to psychoanalysis and in his use and then rejection of methods such as electrotherapy and psychopharmacology.

All these themes have cycled through the history of counseling and psychotherapy and will likely continue to do so in the future.

Second, it is important to understand that there has been much misunderstanding of Freud's clinical guidelines as opposed to his actual clinical practices. Finally, I suggest that it is helpful to group Freud's techniques into two modes, cognitive interpretation and analysis, and empathic attunement.

Recall that we have said that Freud took extant concepts and reworked them into his theory. To take a crucial example, he took the concept of the unconscious and converted it into the bedrock of psychoanalysis—people are fundamentally motivated by ideas, urges, and wishes that lie outside our awareness in our unconscious. In doing so, he discarded certain portions of the original idea, added new facets, and ultimately made it his own. We have already seen how Freud regarded Breuer's work with Anna O. as primarily one of the cathartic method, by which the recall of upsetting experiences produced a curative release of emotions.

The Return of Catharsis

If we take a step back and survey the history of the field of counseling and psychotherapy, we can see how it periodically returns to catharsis—one can make the argument that the therapeutic encounter groups of the 1960s and 1970s were predicated on the idea of the curative elements of catharsis, as well as the "rebirthing" movement of the 1980s and 1990s. While catharsis has played an important role in counseling and psychotherapy, there is a strong theoretical rationale that states that while catharsis may be an important part of therapeutic change and may be valued by clients, catharsis alone, without a cognitive component that allows an individual to derive meaning from the experience and apply it in daily life, is likely transitory in its effects (Yalom, 2005). And so the field continues to return periodically to the concept of catharsis, which had been inaugurated by Freud and Breuer's work in the late 1800s.

The Return of Rest Cures, Electrotherapy, and Psychopharmacology

The same is also true for other techniques. When Freud began his clinical practice in the 1886, he initially "relied on such currently recommended methods of treatment as hydrotherapy, electro-therapy, massage and the Weir Mitchell rest-cure" (Strachey, 1955, p. xi). Hydrotherapy, spas, and rest cures continued throughout the early 1900s (Shorter, 1997)—and it could be argued that while hydrotherapy and the rest cure are no longer widely accepted clinical practices, the general public clearly regards rest and water treatments (whether at spas or the use of private hot tubs) as both physically and mentally therapeutic. Freud used massage in early cases such as Emily Von N. and used his hand to apply pressure on a patient's forehead (Breuer & Freud, 1893–1895/1955), but again, while Freud rejected these methods through the development of psychoanalysis, it can be suggested that massage treatment, along with rest cures and spa treatments, continue to be regarded by the lay public as not just physically beneficial but psychologically beneficial as well.

As Freud (1925/1959) relates when he was just starting out, electrotherapy was one of the few weapons in his "therapeutic arsenal" (p. 16). Fascinatingly, the use of mild forms of electrotherapy in the late 1800s was often directed at the throat toward the "globus hystericus," or difficulties of speech associated with hysteria—the lump in the throat sensation that many of us have experienced in varying degrees. Even more sensationally, mild electrical charges were used during the last part of the 19th and early 20th centuries in genitally stimulating women who were seen as suffering from sexual hysteria: "Genital stimulation via massage and electrotherapy was called 'local massage' or 'local friction,' referring to the application of manual massage, hydro-massage, the mechanical vibrator, or electrical charge directly to the pelvic, genital or rectal local region responsible for the hysterical reflex" (Starr & Aron, 2011, p. 379). There is no evidence that Freud himself engaged in genital stimulation of his early patients, but it is important to understand the context of Freud's early clinical practices and to understand the genesis of electrotherapy within such misogynistic confines that regarded women's sexuality as a medical problem to be "cured."

Electrotherapy waned for a time, but there was a resurgence of interest in the early and mid-1900s; this resurgence led to the abuses of shock treatment so vividly captured in *One Flew Over the Cuckoo's Nest,* which led to the precipitous decline of shock treatments...which led to the re-emergence of a chastened form of electrotherapy, electro-convulsive therapy, or ECT, which is currently used as a treatment for severe and persistent depression. Additionally, there has been recent returning interest in treating depression through the stimulation of the vagal nerve, which runs through the neck! (See Gilman, 2008, for a good short account of the history of electrotherapy.) Electrotherapy is another good example of how important it is to be vigilant and self-reflective about currently accepted clinical practices.

Psychopharmacology makes its conspicuous debut in Freud's early work as well. Freud experimented with cocaine both in his professional and his personal life, prescribing it in the 1880s as "panacea for pain, exhaustion, low spirits, and morphine addiction" (Gay, 2006, p. 44) as well as personally using it as a method of combating anxiety in social settings, such as when he visited the famous Charcot in 1886. Again, while Freud himself repudiated cocaine as a treatment, and led the field in general away from somatic explanations and somatic treatments of mental illness, the field's use of psychopharmacology has waxed and waned and waxed—from the use of morphine and chloral hydrate in the earliest treatment of Anna O. by Breuer, to a relatively quiescent time, to the rise first of benzodiazepine use—Valium, "mother's little helper"—and the explosive growth of antipsychotic and antidepressant medications that gives no indication of slowing.

You Are Getting Very Sleepy...

We should also return to the role of hypnotism in the development of Freud's technique.

As Ellenberger (1970) masterfully demonstrates, mesmerists and hypnotists had long been interacting sympathetically with people; they even knew something about the power of the relationship, which was termed *rapport.* But for those who preceded Freud, there was an element of the magical in the reactions of subjects to those who mesmerized and hypnotized them. As Freud perceptively saw, however, it wasn't magical; it was simply a very human response shown to those who took you seriously and gave you focused attention, concern, and benevolent kindness.

Hypnotism thus serves as the bridge from the earliest forms of therapeutic interventions, such as those enacted by shamans and priests, to more modern forms such as psychoanalysis. It can also serve as yet another example of the cyclical nature of therapeutic techniques and interventions. Hypnotism, with its rapport between subject and hypnotist, was used by Freud in his early practice and rejected as he groped his way toward psychoanalysis proper. To review, Freud rejected it because he came to believe that therapeutic change came about through the arduous task of bringing previously unknown parts of one's psyche into conscious awareness.

Moreover, to Freud, hypnotism carried with it an element of authoritarianism. He says that hypnotic and suggestive methods make use of authority and may in fact "seek to remould him [the client] in accordance with his own—that is, according to the physician's—personal ideals" (Freud, 1923/1955, p. 251). Freud, through the use of techniques that we will examine shortly—the analysis of the transferential relationship, free association, dream interpretation, the analysis of slips of the tongue, and the interpretation of client behavior more generally, thought that he had the necessary techniques to use without resorting to the "mystical ally" (Freud, 1909–1910/1961, p. 20) of hypnosis.

So for all these reasons, Freud rejected hypnosis. And what happened? Did hypnotism, once so prevalent in the 19th century, now tossed into the closet by Freud, cease to exist? On the contrary, it returned. It may be a simplification to say that Milton Erickson singlehandedly revived hypnotism, but not by much. Erickson's oracular pronouncements and the weird, wonderful cures that he devised became famous through devotees such as Haley (1986), who described Erickson as a clinician who saw great value in nonrational, intuitive approaches. Significantly, Erickson modified the traditional way of looking at hypnosis as a formal thing that is done in specific ways ("Look at my watch swing back and forth, you are getting very sleepy...") to understanding that there is a gradual continuum of less and more hypnogogic activities. He helped us understand the many subtle gradations of hypnotic influence, which he called *trance induction*.

No Wait—Your Eyes Aren't Closing—They Are Moving!

And when Erickson's star faded, hypnotism faded as well—only to be reilluminated by intense interest in a magical new technique, Eye Movement Desensitization Reprogramming (EMDR) (Shapiro, 1989, 1995), which employed hypnotic hand and eye movements. At least one critic thought that EMDR was a simple repackaging of mesmerism (McNally, 1999), and later research found that, while it appears to be effective for PTSD, the role of eye movements (which was the centerpiece of the initial technique) might in fact be inessential (Spiegler & Guevremont, 2010). The powerful rhetoric of EMDR parallels that of mesmerism (Justman, 2011), and it is to be suspected that the real potency of EMDR was—as should be apparent by now—found in how the excited and enthusiastic EMDR counselors "infected" their clients with hope and expectancy for change within the counseling relationship—in other words, through common factors, not specific ingredients. Hypnotism, or trance induction, or desensitization reprogramming, or whatever the latest terms are, seems to appear as regularly as a comet in the firmament above the helping professions.

In addition to the necessity of looking at the development of technique within a historical context, it is important to realize that there are numerous conflicts between what Freud suggested we should do as clinicians, how Freud's writings were interpreted by later followers, as well as what we know of Freud's actual clinical practices. We need to tread very carefully here so that we take away a full and nuanced position on a number of crucial points.

Say Everything

Let us start with two points that can be considered for the sake of our present discussion to be hard and fast rules. Freud (1913/2002) says that there is one fundamental prescription that the patient must follow: "you should say everything that comes in to your head" (p. 56). In attempting to say everything that comes into his or her head, the patient invariably pauses or hesitates—and these are precisely the moments that the analyst is interested in, because they signal that there may be disturbing information that is hesitating to come to the surface. When a patient pauses, he or she demonstrates a severed or disrupted association, a blip on the radar screen that might indicate that something large is swimming below the surface of a patient's consciousness.

No Sex With Clients

Freud also is clear throughout his writing that sexual abstinence is expected. However, it is important to look closely at Freud's reasoning why an analyst should refrain from having sex with a patient. Freud (1915/2002) makes it clear that if an analyst exploited the situation in order "to requite the patient's love and satisfy her need for affection" (p. 73)—that is, have sex—"it would be a great triumph for the patient to have her offer of love requited, and a total defeat for the therapy" (p. 73). Freud's reasoning is easy to follow—in gratifying the client's needs, the counselor would be simply playing a role in the tragedy that the client has brought to treatment—"in the course of the love affair she would display all the inhibitions and unhealthy reactions of her erotic life, with no chance of correcting them, and it would end in regret and a greatly reinforced tendency to repression" (p. 73).

Clients generally don't come to counseling because they are thrilled with the choices they have made in their interpersonal relationships, especially their intimate and sexual ones; if they are involved in an intimate and sexual relationship with their counselor, they will very likely reenact the dysfunctional patterns that contribute to their unhappiness—within the relationship in which they were supposed to get help on these dysfunctional patterns! It is no wonder that counselor/client sex is so damaging, resulting in reactions like ambivalence, cognitive issues, emotional ups and downs, feelings of isolation and emptiness, a decreased ability to trust, feelings of guilt, elevated suicide risk, boundary issues, sexual confusion, and anger that is often suppressed (Pope, 2001). Thus Freud (1915/2002) says that "the course of therapy must be conducted on terms of abstinence" (p. 72).

To What Degree Must We Abstain?

No sex with clients—that part is clear. But here is where things get a little confusing. While Freud is very clear on not engaging in sex with clients, he also says that abstinence doesn't mean just sexual abstinence, but that it also means potentially denying a wide range of client demands, wishes, and needs. How far should an analyst go in denying these desires? Well, if we hold that the therapeutic relationship is always in danger of becoming just like other relationships in a client's life, especially unsatisfying ones, then it would seem that the counselor needs to be ever watchful and vigilant about giving in too easily and gratifying clients' desires, even seemingly innocuous and ordinary ones like the need for a little praise or affirmation. Sometimes Freud (1915/2002) sounds suspicious of the patient, and warns us of the dangers of letting ourselves "drift into feelings of affection for the patient" (p. 72).

This Freud—the abstemious, denying, withholding Freud—is a version that many of his followers picked up on. In this version, analysts deflect any and all questions into their personal lives, even seemingly innocuous or innocent ones. The concept of abstinence—which came to be seen as the analyst being opaque, objective, and nongratifying—was enshrined in psychoanalytic lore; the irony is, however, that Freud himself frequently violated this concept in his own clinical work. If one reads accounts written by his patients, such as found in Hilda Doolittle (1956), Lohser and Newton (1996), and Ruitenbeek (1973), one sees numerous examples of Freud being generous and open with his patients (He actually gave money to some of them and gave free treatment to others—and in the case of Hilda Doolittle, he kept trying to give her one of the puppies from Yofi, his beloved Chow dog!). He could frequently miss the boat when he followed his own interpretations rather than attending more closely to his clients, but he was generally attentive and took seriously what his patients said. And it is clear that in being attentive and warmly personal, Freud helped his patients. Thus we have the irony that, in the words of one biographer, "Freud's published papers on technique prohibit the very activities—personal support, praise, friendly interactions, the giving of gifts—that were involved in successful therapeutic outcomes, while recommending the methods—abstinence, anonymity, silence—that were unhelpful and damaging" (Breger, 2001, p. 373).

Recommendations, Not Rules

So Freud himself gives some contradictory advice on crucial aspects of the therapeutic relationship; it can be confusing about whether these are in fact hard and fast rules or simply guidelines. Thompson (1994) makes the important point that with only a few exceptions—sexual abstinence and the rule of saying everything that comes to mind—Freud only made recommendations, not rules, for clinical practice, saying that "his recommendations about the practice of analysis were uncommonly flexible by today's standards. Many of his rules simply reflected his personality, and he told us why. We, in turn, are invited to do the same. But at the same time, we are admonished to use our heads" (p. xxiii). When Freud (1913/2002) did give his rules of psychoanalytic treatment, he said that "it is just as well if I offer these rules as 'advice' and make no binding claims for them" (p. 45), which is not at all how many of his later followers took them. There was a general movement to cast Freud's pronouncements in stone, but Freud's own views were that they should be regarded no more than as advice.

Thoughts and Feelings

Finally, I suggest that Freud's technique can be classified into two modes—cognitive interpretation and analysis, and affective attunement. Regarding cognition, Freud (1927/1961) valued the power of the intellect, the last good hope of reason: "the voice of the intellect is a soft one, but it does not rest till it has gained a hearing. Finally, after a countless succession of rebuffs, it succeeds" (p. 53). The Ego is, however imperfectly and however laggardly, capable of reasonable, rational operations. While it can be deluged with the Id's passions, buffeted by criticism from the Superego, and cowed by an uncaring outer world, still the Ego can think about its experience of the world and test its perceptions of reality. From a modern standpoint, it is the seat of executive function—the human ability to plan ahead, formulate hypotheses, analyze and integrate memories, and so forth.

But Freud clearly also valued empathic attunement—the metaphor of the unconscious as an instrument attuned to the patient's unconscious. Freud valued *takt*—tact—highly and a kind of commonsense empathic attunement that made the patient feel at ease and trustful of the analyst (Thompson, 1994). Without this attunement, patients do not feel heard and understood.

Freud could use much psychoanalytic jargon when describing the curative aspects of analysis, but he also could be blunt—in a letter to Jung, he says that "you are probably aware that our cures are brought about through the fixation of the libido prevailing in the unconscious (transference)"—classic Freudian jargon—before going on to say that "essentially, one might say, the cure is effected by love" (McGuire, 1979, p. 10). It bears repeating—Freud used the word *love* to describe how the psychoanalytic cure was brought about—a far cry from the vision of the unempathic and distant figure that has been enshrined in psychoanalytic lore. Though Freud believed that psychoanalysis should be founded on scientific principles, and from Jung's (1961) viewpoint, was excessively rational and disparaged intuition, Freud in fact frequently acknowledged that psychoanalysis was as much art as science and made much use of affective information and judgments, as the above quotation illustrates. In his advice to practitioners, he gives much leeway and leaves the exact details to the individual analyst, clearly articulating a flexible policy that allowed the analyst to follow her or his hunches, hypotheses that should be rationally based, but subject to information gathered using empathic attunement.

Quick Clinical Vignette

The Mother and the Man

One of the clearest clinical examples of how empathic attunement and cognitive interpretations are vitally interrelated was furnished for me in my work with a young man who had suffered a psychotic episode. It had been his first, and the interdisciplinary team at the clinic where I worked were gathering information to help him and his family adjust and cope and look ahead to potential treatment options. He was exhibiting classic symptoms of disordered speech and had exhibited disorganized and alarming behavior, such as smearing his own feces on the walls and making sexual advances to his sister.

While I was seeing him in one session, he began to visibly fall apart. The young man had formed a good connection with our staff psychiatrist, who was an incredibly skilled and compassionate clinician, so I asked if he would feel safe walking with me down the hall to visit with him. He agreed.

The young man's speech was pressured and disorganized and he continually returned to the themes of his mother (his mother didn't have pillow breasts—women should have pillow breasts—his mother is skinny as a cow) and of a figure who was persecuting him (The Man).

The young man's speech reached a crescendo, and he said, "Skinny Mom doesn't rest me on her breasts, the Man tests me and tests me, he reels me in and throws me out and reels me in and throws me out!"

The psychiatrist gently looked into the young man's eyes and said, "Would you like us to reel you in?" The young man sobbed, heartbreakingly, "Yes," and we later readmitted him to the hospital.

This psychiatrist achieved, in that heartrending moment, the most intense affective attunement I've witnessed. He paired it with an exceptionally acute interpretation, one in which he accurately understood what the client was telling us: that his mom wasn't nurturing and protecting him in a way that he needed to be nurtured and protected (his mother was, in fact, very compassionate and loving, but was understandably overwhelmed by her son's behavior); that he was being pursued by an incredibly scary experience (presumably his experience of psychosis); and that he was asking us to step in and protect him from this scary experience. The takeaway is that as we consider Freud's techniques and methods, we should bear in mind the way in which the two modes of affective attunement and accurate, interpretive understanding complement one another in effective treatment.

The Tools of Psychoanalysis: Interventions to Accomplish Its Aim

To review, Freud said that the Ego develops, from birth, within the context of a continual struggle to balance the demands of reality, the Id, and the Superego. Some individuals develop a resilient and capable Ego that succeeds, if not perfectly, at least reasonably well in harmonizing these demands. Others succeed less well, and experience isolated or chronic periods when these relations break down and the Ego abandons its task and symptoms result.

First, Ally With the Ego

The strategy for treatment, Freud (1940/1964) tells us, consists of the analyst allying with the client's beleaguered Ego, forming a pact that they will try to figure out how to meet the real demands of the external world and not give in blindly to the urgent, raw demands of the Id or the harsh, accusatory criticisms of the Superego. Remember that as the terms of this pact, "the sick ego promises us the most complete candour—promises, that is, to put at our disposal all the material which its self-perception yields it" (Freud, 1940/1964, p. 173). Remember that the analyst asks the client to "obey the *fundamental rule* of analysis...he is to tell us not only what he can say intentionally and willingly, what will give him relief like a confession, but everything else as well that his self-observation yields him, everything that comes into his head, even if it is *disagreeable* for him to say it, even if it seems to him *unimportant* or actually *nonsensical*" (p. 174). In doing so, the client will provide important information about his or her unconscious—disguised and transformed material, but important nonetheless. The analyst thus is in the position of helping the client rationally examine this material and choosing what to do about it.

But here's the rub: "the patient is not satisfied with regarding the analyst in the light of reality as a helper and adviser...on the contrary, the patient sees in him the return, the reincarnation, of some important figure out of his childhood or past, and consequently transfers on to him feelings and reactions which undoubtedly applied to this prototype" (Freud, 1940/1964, p. 174). The Ego does not welcome the new information, precisely because this new information is painful and deeply upsetting—remember that the very reason it was pushed out of conscious awareness was that it was too hard for the Ego to handle.

To understand this situation, think about something that is very difficult for you to tolerate. Think about a painful rejection from your childhood, when you were rejected by a friend or a family member. Now understand that from a Freudian perspective, this is only pain that you are able to remember; there were other thoughts and ideas so painful that they were immediately pushed out of your conscious awareness and in fact still remain so. When, through analysis, you are beginning to become aware of this painful material, you don't simply accept it, but instead you tend to reexperience it. Part of this reexperiencing means that you will treat the person who is helping you reexperience it like a person from your past.

So clients, to varying degrees, will treat the analyst as a past figure, often a parental one. In doing so, they will also tend to put themselves in the position of children who want love and acceptance from their parents. Negatively, they may push aside their primary reason to be in treatment—to get better—in order to gain this love and approval. If getting worse means more care and attention from their counselor, then so be it. Or they may get better not for their own sake, but to win approval from their counselor. Or they may react not with love, but with hate. In the context of treatment, powerful unconscious material is unearthed, which makes the client feel vulnerable. Feeling vulnerable, the client may regress to psychological states associated with childhood, one of which may be a desire for the counselor, in the role of all-powerful parent, to take away all their hurt and pain—to kiss the boo-boo and magically make it all better. When the counselor inevitably fails to do so, the client may react with rage—"he hates the analyst as his enemy and is ready to abandon the analysis" (Freud, 1940/1964, p. 176).

Transference, Pros and Cons

But as we have seen, Freud came to regard the negative aspects of transference as being vastly outweighed by the positives. As long as the clinician is aware of the potency of the relationship and is cognizant of the possible negative reactions on the part of the client, transference conveys crucial advantages that can be used in treatment. In the first place, "if the patient puts the analyst in the place of his father (or mother), he is also giving him the power which his super-ego exercises over his ego, since his parents were, as we know, the origin of his super-ego. The new super-ego now has an opportunity for a sort of *after-education* of the neurotic; it can correct mistakes for which his parents were responsible for educating him" (Freud, 1940/1964, p. 175).

The potency of the therapeutic relationship can be vastly enhanced when a client treats you like a past paternal or maternal figure—they are giving you the opportunity of gently correcting mistakes that were made in the client's upbringing. Remember that the Superego tends to incorporate harsh parental demands; a clinical corollary would be that the clinician needs to be exquisitely sensitive to ways in which the client might perceive them as critical and to tactfully and compassionately examine this response. Additionally, Freud makes the important point that the clinician must be very careful and very respectful of client autonomy. The client may wish us to be "teacher, model and ideal" (Freud, 1940/1964, p. 175) but we must be very careful to avoid misusing our influence, because if a counselor does so, "he will only be repeating a mistake of the parents who crushed their child's independence by their influence, and he will only be replacing the patient's earlier dependence by a new one" (p. 175).

Another important benefit of transference is how it "produces before us with plastic clarity an important part of his life-story, of which he would otherwise have probably given us only an insufficient account. He acts it before us, as it were, instead of reporting it to us" (Freud, 1940/1964, p. 176). As we have seen, everything about the therapeutic encounter potentially tells us important information about a client's past and present relationships, and this information is real-time and immediately available for discussion. In fact, as we see further in the chapter on later developments, the relational aspects of treatment have come to dominate psychoanalytic thought and practice. And exciting developments in neuroscience further buttress the idea that psychotherapy furnishes an ideal context for reenacting past and present interpersonal relationships with a view toward cognitive restructuring and emotional readjustment. The remaining analytic techniques of free associations, dream analysis, and the famous Freudian slips are understood to be used within the context of the transferential relationship.

Free Association

As we have seen with free association, it is the fundamental rule—say whatever comes to mind—and also, paradoxically, what doesn't come to mind. Something special is asked of the client—to trust the therapeutic relationship enough to risk not only saying what is acceptable in polite company, but also what is unacceptable. This is furthermore complicated by the knowledge that the client must say everything to the clinician—and to the clinician in the role of parent. It becomes easy to understand why the client would resist producing such charged material—and to understand how vital it is for the clinician to fully understand the risk that is being asked of the client—as well as the potential for cure simply from being allowed to say anything and everything that comes to mind. One contemporary psychoanalytic practitioner believes that the sole difference between her successful and unsuccessful cases is whether her clients were able to follow this fundamental cure: "Saying everything is the key to successful analysis" (Holmes, 2008, p. 71).

There is something special asked of the clinician as well. As we have seen, there is an important ethical imperative to follow: the clinician must be careful not to overstep boundaries and unreflectively take on the role of the parent. Additionally, Freud (1912/2002) tells us that as the client produces unconscious material, the clinician must listen with a kind of "impartially suspended attention" (p. 33) that seeks to lay aside preconceived notions and instead be immersed in the client's unconscious material. He says that clinicians must hear the material in a way that parallels how clients produce it. The clinician must avoid substituting his own censorship of the client's material, but instead "he should orientate his own unconscious, as a kind of receptive organ, towards the communicative unconscious of the patient" (p. 37), functioning like a receiver that transforms sound waves into recognizable speech. The clinician must obey the rule in order to not introduce his or her own distortions, which would inevitably muddle up the material produced by the client.

Dream Analysis

These rules govern dream analysis as well. In listening to clients recounting their dreams, analysts need to listen in a correspondingly dreamlike state—one in which their receptive unconscious is receiving signals from the clients' unconscious with clarity and without distortions. Dreams furnish wonderful opportunities to get in contact with a client's unconscious desires; they are as close we can get to experiencing the unconscious, so it is no wonder that Freud (1909–1910/1961) famously said that "the interpretation of dreams is in fact the royal road to a knowledge of the unconscious" (p. 33); he also said that his best advice to the question How can I become a psychoanalyst? is to study one's own dreams. It should come as no surprise that this is indeed how Freud himself began psychoanalysis—by studying his own dreams in *The Interpretation of Dreams*.

Freud was very sensitive to the fact that dream interpretation had a long and somewhat suspect history, being used for superstitious purposes in ancient religions and societies, and in *Five Lectures* he admits that he held off talking about dreams until the third lecture because he thought that Americans, known for their practicality and no-nonsense approach to life, might regard him as bit of charlatan if he started with dream interpretation. But dreams, in Freud's view, do more than just preserve sleep or review the activities of one's day. Instead they furnish us with important information about some of our deepest concerns. In Freud's (1900/1953a) formulation, "*a dream is a (disguised) fulfillment of a (suppressed or repressed) wish*" (p. 160). In other words, dreams convey, in sometimes bizarre form, information about some of our deepest longings and desires. But, as we have emphasized, these desires are often so primitive, and so unacceptable, that even in the state of lowered defensiveness that we find ourselves when we sleep, we cannot fully accept them and thus our dreams disguise them for us. The work for the analyst, then, is to help a client understand how a particular dream might symbolize certain deep-seated conflicts. In the receptive state of evenly suspended attention, clinicians can begin to sense the real person hiding underneath the fantastic garb of dreams.

Slips of the Tongue, Jokes, and Habitual Actions

Like dreams, slips and jokes and habitual actions and gestures also represent unguarded moments in conscious mental life. Freud (1905/1960) compared and contrasted the function of dreams and jokes, finding much in common. He said that in dreams, the processes of representation (by which material is represented in sensory images), condensation (by which there is a telegraphic conveyance of a great deal of related material), and displacement (by which the relative importance, for instance, of material is switched so that the unimportant becomes important) are quite similar to the same processes in jokes. Jokes describes sometimes absurd images (A dog walks into a bar and orders a drink...), they condense huge amounts of related material (What's the difference between men and women? Men...and women...), and they displace our expectations and start us on entirely new trains of thought (Take my mother-in-law—Please.)

In jokes, the material that comics present us with is the unexpressed material of our unconscious. And what do comics joke about? Do they joke about what kind and gentle and sensitive people we are underneath. Hardly. Comedians reveal to us that our unconscious thoughts are gluttonous, lustful, racist, sexist, murderous, and so on. These comics force recognition in us—when we bark and howl with laughter, we are delighted and relieved—*someone said what we really think! I'm not the only one with these unacceptable thoughts about people who are different than I am! I can admit that I have these views too and I'm not necessarily a horrible person!* It might be said that humor allows for the safe release of a certain amount of sexual and aggressive energy through laughter. And from a Freudian point of view, the comedians who you *don't* think are funny, might be precisely those comics who are trying to tell you about things in your unconscious that you don't want to hear.

The famous Freudian slips and other verbal miscues also point to the existence of unconscious material that cannot, due to psychical censorship, come out in direct form but come out sideways. And not just verbal, but behavior such as "playing about and fiddling with things, humming tunes, fingering parts of one's own body or one's clothing and so on" (Freud, 1909–1910/1961, p. 39). In all such verbal and nonverbal activity, we find that it "can be traced back to incompletely suppressed psychical material, which, although pushed away by consciousness, has nonetheless not been robbed of all capacity for expressing itself" (Freud, 1901/1960, p. 279). Dreams, along with speech and nonverbal behavior, have rich meanings which can be indicative of our individual and societal unconscious preoccupations.

Rounding Out the Picture: King Oedipus, Sex/Love and Aggression/Death, the Nature of Trauma, and Other Freudian Controversies

Freud believed that the story of King Oedipus told us about the central motivations of a man's life. This is one of the wild claims that critics such as McNally (2006) admonished him for. *Really?* They ask. *Every boy unconsciously wants to kill his father and marry his mother? That's ridiculous!*

Let's briefly examine the Oedipus story before going on to see if it holds any practical utility. In the story, King Laius and Queen Jocasta of Thebes have a child, Oedipus. It is prophesized that any child born to Laius will kill him. In an attempt to evade the prophecy, Laius abandons the child on a mountain; however, Oedipus is rescued and is raised by King Polybus and Queen Merope. Later, when Oedipus is grown, he also finds out about the prophecy that he is destined to kill his father, so he flees those whom he thinks are his parents, Polybus and Merope. He encounters his biological father Laius on the road, and in a conflict with him, kills him. Oedipus comes to Thebes and vanquishes the Sphinx that has been terrorizing the people there. He marries his biological mother Jocasta, and they have children.

Eventually, Oedipus finds out that he indeed fulfilled the prophecy: unknowingly, he killed his father and married his mother.

Could This Story Tell Us Anything About Freud?

Now we can approach this story a number of ways; since we are "doing Freud" in this book, let's first ask ourselves, What could have possibly motivated Freud to postulate this story as the prime motivation for all mankind? Could there have possibly been something in his childhood that might give us some insight? Take a wild guess—do you think that Freud might have harbored murderous thoughts about his father and lustful thoughts about his mother?

The answer is, of course, yes. He did in fact have a vivid memory of seeing his mother naked—this vision was so striking that when he talked about it to his colleague, Wilhelm Fliess, he used the Latin words for *mother* and *naked* (Masson, 1985). Think about it: Freud, a man for whom it was so important to talk in a matter-of-fact way about sex, to remove superstition and ignorance and guilt from it, had to use the dead language of Latin to describe his mother—a mother who, we know, was quite voluptuous and beautiful in young Sigmund's eyes. Do we think that he might be repressing something of a sexual nature here?

He also shared, in *The Interpretation of Dreams,* a vivid memory that is highly revealing of his attitude toward his father: when he was a young boy, he came into his parents' bedroom at night and urinated in front of them (presumably into a chamber pot, though I like to envision the little Sigmund peeing into a potted palm). When he did it, his father said, "The boy will come to nothing" (Freud, 1900/1953a, p. 216). To imagine Sigmund's reaction, we must realize that one of Freud's most enduring and powerful personal characteristics was his incredible drive and ambition (Gay, 2006). This was a boy who dreamed of becoming great, of changing the world, of being mentioned in the same breath as Galileo, who saw himself as a scientific conquistador. Imagine that you have powerful fantasies that you will conquer the world—and your father tells your mother that you are going to come to nothing. What do you feel? Murderous rage, perhaps?

Sex, Sex, and Sex

Thus, if we use the very tools that Freud gives us to analyze why he assigned such importance to a story about a man who kills his father and has sex with his mother, we can see what might have motivated Freud. But is that all that it is useful for—to reveal Freud's preoccupations? I suggest that there are several ways in which it remains useful. First, it is important to recognize that father and mother can serve as powerful objects and symbols of feelings of aggression and sexuality. In fact, it's quite common for young children to say that they want to marry their father or mother—or that they hate them and wish they were dead. But obviously for many if not most people, this aspect is not of ongoing vital concern; it appears to be indeed one of the famous phases that we tend to grow out of. Yes, there may be an aspect of sexuality and aggression in our relationship to our parents, but it doesn't usually appear to be of such concern that it need be postulated as the overriding clinical objective. Like extreme feelings of love and hate in the therapeutic relationship, it is uncommon to experience murderous rage or sexual lust for one's parents; however, just as with the therapeutic relationship, it is important for the clinician to realize the potential for such feelings to exist.

Second, Freud fundamentally expanded our ideas of what, in fact, sex is. Freud (1910/2002) said that "in psychoanalysis, the concept of sexuality certainly embraces much more; in both higher and lower senses it reaches beyond the popular meaning. This extension is justified in terms of the human genetic heritage; for us, 'sexual life' includes everything that prompts those tender feelings deriving from the original source of primitive sexual impulses, even if those impulses have been subjected to inhibitions placed on their original sexual aims, or if they have exchanged these aims for others that are no longer sexual. That is why we prefer to talk about psychosexuality, and thus stress the importance of not overlooking or underestimating the emotional factor in sexual life. We employ the word sexuality in the same broad sense as the German language uses the word 'lieben' [love]" (pp. 4–5). We can understand, perhaps, how sexuality is like loving—in English, of course, we speak of "making love," but he also says that our sexual lives include things that are no longer recognizable as sexual. He says that we must not forget our genetic heritage—our linkages with the natural world, but also our unique and frankly bizarre ability to turn sexual desire into opera and fashion and chocolate and sports and...

And this expansion of our understanding of sexuality occurs naturally if we look to the beginning of human life itself: "a child has its sexual instincts and activities from the first; it comes into the world with them; and, after an important course of development passing through many stages, they lead what is known as the normal sexuality of the adult" (Freud, 1909–1910/1961, p. 44). It's all there, if only we look for it: "There is no difficulty in observing the manifestations of these sexual activities in children; on the contrary, it calls for some skill to overlook them or explain them away" (p. 44). Freud understood why "most people (whether medical observers or others) will hear nothing of the sexual life of children. They have forgotten their own infantile sexual activity under the pressure of their education to a civilized life, and they do not wish to be reminded of what has been repressed" (p. 46). It's there, but we just don't want to see it. It's a hard thing to hear, that our sexuality has such a literally infantile origin. It's not something that any of us would like to hear—that the expression of adult sexuality grows out of the infantile. But Freud (1905/1953) never lets us forget it, and in one famous passage, he says that "no one who has seen a baby sinking back satiated from the breast and falling asleep with flushed cheeks and a blissful smile can escape the reflection that this picture persists as the prototype of the expression of sexual satisfaction in later life" (p. 182). Ouch. In the adult human sexual act we find the baby, with a blissful smile on its face and milk on its chin.

According to Freud, the primitive and regressed nature of many sexual fantasies and desires are so much better explained when we choose to see rather than to ignore the connection between adult and infantile experiences. Remember that he said that all children have an innate aptitude for being "polymorphously perverse" (Freud, 1905/1953, p. 191) in which they can, through early sexualization, become oriented in all kinds of ways to all kinds of sexual objects and activities. The variety of human sexuality again has its origins in what it means to grow and develop as a human being, either in ways that protect and nurture the expression of sexuality, or ways that tend to confuse and limit it.

Sex and Violence

Finally, there is yet another way in which Freud's central concerns—sexual urges, along with aggressive and violent ones—point us toward another vital theme, that of sexual violence. Sexual violence is a central preoccupation of our field. But what is not as well known is that Freud originally thought that a particular kind of sexual trauma—the early and inappropriate sexualization of children—caused *all* forms of neurosis. Originally, Freud (1896/1962a) said that "at the bottom of every case of hysteria there are one or more occurrences of premature sexual experiences" (p. 203) and he cites eighteen cases—six men and twelve women—that revealed early childhood sexual experience. Freud (1925/1959) later said that "with female patients the part of seducer was almost always assigned to their father. I believed these stories, and consequently supposed that I had discovered the roots of the subsequent neurosis in these experiences of sexual seduction in childhood" (p. 34). This theory has been termed Freud's seduction theory, and it was his first formulation of the origins of neuroses.

Crucially, however, he changed his mind. He came to believe that what patients told him about did not happen in fact—that "the neurotic symptoms were not related directly to actual events but to wishful phantasies" (p. 34). Freud had a variety of reasons for changing his mind (Gay, 1989b). Clinically, he didn't seem to be getting anywhere with these clients—though he uncovered this childhood sexual trauma, it didn't seem to help them. Logically, it seemed to be an impossibility that all neurosis was caused by sexual trauma—sexual trauma would have to be incredibly widespread, since it stood to reason that not every single person who had experienced sexual trauma went on to develop a neurosis, but only those where "there has been an accumulation of events and where a factor that weakens defence" (p. 112) came into play. Additionally, he wondered how one could know what really happened—the question of how reliable any of us can be, when relating early childhood experiences. And, crucially, since the father was invariably implicated, that meant that even his own father "had to be blamed as a pervert" (p. 112).

Critics such as Masson (1984) have blasted Freud's abandonment of the seduction theory, saying that in doing so he did the field, and childhood sexual abuse victims, a huge disservice. These critics say that Freud in effect denied the experience of child sexual abuse victims, telling them *it's all in your head, you made it up, it never happened*. In reality, Freud (1925/1959) never fully abandoned the idea that actual sexual trauma existed, but he did say that it played a much humbler role than what he originally envisioned. This shift was a momentous one, ranking with his other technique-oriented shifts as a fundamental change in his approach.

IMPORTANT MODIFICATIONS MADE BY FREUD

Freud modified his thinking as his career developed. Some of these modifications were relatively minor; others were major. Major modifications include the following:

- Moving from catharsis ("let it all out") to psychoanalysis proper (make the unconscious conscious; make rational decisions about newly conscious material)
- Rejecting hypnotism in favor of free association, dream interpretation, and transference analysis
- Starting in relative ignorance of the power of therapeutic relationship to an awareness of the power of that relationship—and how to make constructive use of it
- Moving from a theory in which actual sexual abuse/trauma/seduction caused mental illness to the idea that people are made sick and/or neurotic through the repression of powerful, unacceptable wishes and/or fantasies—the Oedipal complex. For his theory and his practice, this meant focusing less on the actual events that make people sick (such as abuse in their childhood), and focusing more on their (repressed) feelings and thoughts.

Was Freud Sexualized at an Early Age?

It is fascinating how we can yet again use Freud's techniques in helping us understand his rejection of the seduction theory in more rich detail. There has been speculation that Freud may have been sexualized at an early age. Freud himself recognized neurotic symptoms in himself and in his siblings; according to the seduction theory, his own father would be responsible for their neurotic symptoms—had he sexually abused them? According to this line of reasoning, Freud couldn't accept the idea that his father was a "pervert" and thus had to push out of his awareness this possibility; it was so potent that this happened without his being aware that this was what he was doing. What is this called? Repression.

Interestingly, there is some evidence that Freud's nanny may have sexualized him. Freud did speak cryptically of how she initiated him in a letter to Fliess, saying that she was his "teacher in sexual matters" (Gay, 1989b, p. 114) when he was 2 or 3. Paul Vitz (1988), citing some evidence that in certain cultures caregivers rub the penises of infants to soothe them, speculates that his nurse, who was from a rural and less-educated background, might have done this to Freud. Vitz also suggests that Freud was sexualized by a later servant girl and/or a neighbor girl and/or the landlord's daughter. He goes through evidence (*Screen Memories* and other early writings by Freud, e.g., *Further Remarks on the Defence Neuro-Psychoses*) to suggest that as a result of being sexualized, Freud may have engaged in some sexual play with sisters, probably involving older half-nephew John (John was like an older cousin due to age differences between Freud's father and mother). John might have been seduced by an older nursemaid, and then sexualized Freud, and both might have then sexualized Freud's sister. There are no pieces of unequivocal evidence, but there is some internal support from Freud's life and work that he had undergone early sexualization.

Sexual Trauma

From a clinical standpoint, this discussion is a crucial one. We now have much evidence on childhood sexual trauma. While huge methodological issues remain in determining the actual rates of childhood sexual abuse (including, for instance, how even to define what childhood sexual abuse is/means/includes), we do know that it is sadly prevalent in our society. According to Finkelhor (1994), approximately 20% of all women in North America experienced some form of sexual abuse in childhood, and 5% to 10% of men. It remains an open question how much and to what degree childhood sexual abuse affects us as individuals and as a society, and this open question needs to be asked and answers offered.

It is yet another example of recurring themes: after Freud downgraded the importance of childhood sexual abuse as a cause of neurosis, it lapsed into relative abeyance...to be revived, in part, by the so-called recovered memory movement, which asserted that there had been a cover-up, started by Freud, of childhood sexual abuse (Rush, 1980). It is crucial to know the history—because yet again, the pendulum swung—and according to critics, swung too far—toward locating individual and societal problems in actual childhood sexual abuse. Rush (1980) and the recovered memory movement began to see childhood sexual abuse everywhere; in a truly odd, Freudian move, they began to see it even when people said that it didn't happen to them! (This is the worst kind of Freudian interpretation—when the client says, No, it didn't happen, that actually provides the best evidence that it did happen, because this means that they are showing resistance, which in turn shows that there is repressed material hidden there. In the end, No = Yes.)

So there was a backlash against the idea that we all, at some point, experience sexual abuse but just didn't remember it. And then? There has been a quiet resurgence of empirical research (e.g., Douglas & Finkelhor, 2005; Finkelhor, 1994; Finkelhor & Jones, 2004) that addressed this important issue from a calmer and more objective perspective. So this is another example of the waxing and waning cycles of our field's central preoccupations, which has provoked intense discussion and a hopefully more systemic view of childhood sexual abuse and the need for societal, institutional, and familial guidelines and safeguards to protect children. Yet again, in the development of his theory and his clinical practices, Freud inaugurated one of our field's key themes.

Summary

- In Freud's later structural view, a person's mental life consists of an ongoing struggle; in this struggle, the rational Ego attempts to mediate between unacceptable thoughts and urges—the Id; the critical, internalized parental voices—the Superego; and the real-life demands of the external world.
- This structural perspective can be mapped onto Freud's earlier topographical view of the mind, wherein some operations are inaccessible and can be termed *unconscious*, some operations are latent and can be termed *preconscious*, and some operations are accessible and can be termed *conscious*.
- The Id is wholly unconscious; the Ego and the Superego extend from the conscious into the preconscious and the unconscious.
- A person's development crucially depends on the Ego to successfully mediate in this struggle; problems develop when it abdicates its role.
- Freud's defense mechanisms are patterned ways we respond to perceived threats from without and within.

- The mechanism of repression, wherein distressing material is pushed out of conscious awareness, is deeply dysfunctional—and common. Other defense mechanisms range from relatively less functional to relatively more functional; sublimation is the best option, and in fact is so functional that some don't consider it a defense mechanism but rather a coping mechanism. Yet even sublimation can be overused—Freud encourages us to have fun sometimes, too (*fun* here meaning—what else?—*sex*).
- The treatment aim of Freud's method is simply stated as to **bring unconscious material to conscious awareness, and to strengthen the Ego so that it can make rational judgments about this material.**
- Resistance will be encountered, because the Ego will fear that it can't handle what is being asked of it; the counselor coaches the Ego to get back on the horse.
- Counselors should remember: slow and steady wins the race. The replacement of longstanding, dysfunctional patterns can—and probably should—take time and effort to accomplish.
- Important themes such as hypnosis, electrotherapy, and psychopharmacology continue to return, and the informed counselor should be alert for new iterations on these themes.
- While Freud's therapeutic objectivity (talked about as abstinence) has been enshrined in the literature, in fact his practice was much more complex than has been discussed; he was actually quite personal in his treatment—if he really liked you, he might give you a puppy!
- It can be helpful to consider two modes—affective attunement and cognitive interpretation—as complimentary and necessary in effective treatment.
- Free association, dream analysis, and the analysis of slips and habitual behavior are most fruitfully addressed in the context of the transferential relationship.
- The Oedipus complex encapsulates Freud's reductive strategy; in his view, the most parsimonious (explaining the most phenomena with the least amount of theory) explanation of human behavior is found in the interplay between sexual/erotic drives and urges and aggressive/destructive drives and urges.
- Freud's initial clinical experience led him to suspect that child sexual abuse was the cause of all neuroses; he changed his views, but the importance of sexual trauma has reassumed a prominent place in ongoing counseling efforts.

3

The Evolution of Psychoanalysis

We begin by examining Freud's original drive theory before taking a look at several of the many, many modifications, updates, and revisions of psychoanalytic theory and practice. From a common factors perspective, we have learned the language of psychoanalysis as originally spoken by Freud. But just like any other living language, psychoanalysis's vocabulary and idioms have changed over the years, and we gain a sense of modern usage and how it is being spoken today. As we do so, the reader should bear in mind that it is possible to identify two overarching developments of practical and theoretical significance: (1) the movement from a one-person to a two-and-more-person theory and practice, in which there is a concern for accounting not just for internal drives but also relations with other human beings and the internal representations that we construct of these beings (Greenberg & Mitchell, 1983), and (2) the integration of the latest in neuroscience findings into psychoanalytic theory and practice (Schore, 1994, 2003, 2011). These two modifications—relational approaches and neuroscientific findings—fundamentally define the evolution of psychoanalysis

Freud's Drive Theory

McWilliams (1994) provides a practical, clinically driven approach to making sense of classical psychoanalysis and later formulations. In describing Freud's drive theory, she suggests that "an attempt was made to understand personality on the basis of fixation (at what early developmental phase is this person psychologically stuck?)" (p. 19). That is, do people display issues that suggest they have an oral, anal, phallic, or Oedipal character? If they had been neglected up to the age of 1 and a half, then they might have oral issues; if they had problems from 1 and a half to age 3, they might have typically obsessive anal issues; if their developing interest in sex was not negotiated well between the ages of 3 and 6, they might develop hysterical symptoms and sexual aggression and fantasies that represent Oedipal conflicts; at the onset of puberty, they might display the myriad problems that can develop as one's attention turns from a self-focus to an other-focus.

Freud's theory of developmental stages has undergone many revisions: for more information, please visit the website, http://study.sagepub.com/theoriesforcounselors; and read "Erik Erikson's updates of Freud's developmental stages," which discusses Freud's stages and shows how Erikson's reformulations enhance our understanding and provides for a more clinically useful approach for counselors. What is most important to keep in mind is the overarching point that Freud makes. Remember that Freud said that infants are primarily motivated to seek instinctual gratification—they are all Id, seeking pleasure and satisfaction of their desires; remember that he also said that an essential part of becoming an adult is to realize that one's desires cannot always, or even often, be satisfied exactly how and when we want them to be satisfied.

Becoming an adult, in Freud's view, meant that we must come to see how sublimation—remember this is one of the three possibilities he outlines in *Five Lectures*—is of great value, because it represents a creative and constructive compromise between what I want and what I can have. Society could not exist if we all could get what we wanted, when we wanted it, and how we wanted it. Freud, as should be apparent by now, was quite clear-eyed about the darker side of human nature. There is a sad human history of cruelty, war, and genocide that runs parallel to the human history of kindness, love, and creativity. Freud falls in line with the view that without cultural agreements to dampen and modulate the worst excesses of human desires and lusts, we would exist in a state of lawlessness and chronic warfare, what Thomas Hobbes (1651/2009) described as "a time of Warre, where every man is Enemy to every man" (p. 178). Sublimation, in which we transmute the base metal of our crude desires into the golden achievements of productive work, represents the way in which we can replace unserviceable aims with ones that can benefit both the individual and society at large, and caregivers help accomplish this through helping children take the small steps that ultimately lead to successful sublimation.

The task for caregivers, as McWilliams (1994) describes, is "oscillating sensitively between, on the one hand, sufficient gratification to create emotional security and pleasure and, on the other, developmentally appropriate frustration such that the child would learn in titrated doses how to replace the pleasure principle ('I want all my gratifications, including mutually contradictory ones, right now!') with the reality principle ('Some gratifications are problematic, and the best are worth waiting for')" (p. 21). She goes on to say that "parenting was thus a balancing act between indulgence and inhibition—an intuitively resonant model for most mothers and fathers, to be sure" (p. 21).

A person becomes stuck when they are either overindulged or prevented from enjoying reasonable satisfaction of their desires at key psychosexual developmental stages. Remember, Freud believed that constitutionally people came equipped with stronger or weaker Its/Ids, as well as greater and lesser abilities to regulate them; the caregivers' task is to know their child—the strength of their drives as well as their inborn ability to withstand and regulate these drives—and to skillfully steer the child from being shipwrecked on either the Scylla of overindulgence or the Charybis of intolerable frustration.

Additionally, you should be aware that in Freud's original formulation he did acknowledge the existence and importance of "objects"—that is, other human beings—but that he, and other theorists who tried to preserve the original vision of the drive theory, thought about these objects "largely in relation to the discharge of drive: they may inhibit discharge, facilitate it, or serve as its target" (Greenberg & Mitchell, 1983, p. 3). In this formulation, the developing individual comes to understand others primarily from the point of view of whether they will help me achieve pleasure, prevent me from achieving pleasure, or serve as the object of my pleasure—or frustration. While it is useful to acknowledge that human interaction can be described in part by such a view, it is also highly likely that for most of us, this is entirely too limited a perspective on the incredible complexity of human interaction, and that it is entirely too instrumental, and possibly even cynical, a limitation that later relational theorists corrected, as we shall shortly see.

Ego

It is interesting that a concentration on the Ego is often seen as a later formulation, somehow secondary to Freud's fundamental concerns and methods. However, as Anna Freud (1936/1993) stated very clearly, this is erroneous. She said that "somehow or other" it came to be held that "the term *psychoanalysis* should be reserved for the new discoveries relating to the unconscious psychic life, i.e., the study of repressed instinctual impulses, affects, and fantasies" (p. 3). But she forcefully debunks this idea, saying that the Ego was central all along: "from the beginning analysis, as a therapeutic method, was concerned with the ego and its aberrations: the investigation of the id and of its mode of operation was always only a means to an end. And the end was invariably the same: the correction of these abnormalities and the restoration of the ego to its integrity" (p. 4).

This should sound familiar to you by now, since it restates succinctly and lucidly her father's own ideas on the topic. Thus it is important to understand that while it is common to refer to something called Ego psychology as a later development, in fact it is somewhat nonsensical to do so. The Ego was introduced in conjunction with the Id and the Superego and the external world, as we have seen. It is the dynamic interplay among these players that Freud was concerned with, and I follow Anna Freud's (1936/1993) lead in saying that Freudian analysis's fundamental task was to explore the Ego's "contents, its boundaries, and its functions, and to trace the history of its dependence on the outside world, the id, and the superego; and in relation to the id, to give an account of the instincts, i.e., of the id contents, and to follow them through the transformations which they undergo" (pp. 4–5). If anything, "Ego psychology" could be seen as Anna Freud's correction on an erroneous movement to somehow separate out the Id from the Ego rather than to examine their dynamic interplay.

Object Relations and Interpersonal Psychoanalysis

Greenberg and Mitchell (1983) suggested that while there has been and continues to be much diversity among psychoanalytic theorists and practitioners, "the common 'landscape' of psychoanalysis today consists of an increasing focus on people's interactions with others, that is, on the problem of object relations" (p. 2). Freud thought that people were fundamentally motivated by biological drives; these drives serve as both causes and goals of our thoughts and behaviors. He didn't ignore our relationships with other people, but thought that we are centrally preoccupied with our body-based drives. These drives produce body and mind-based tension, which we try to discharge; when tensions are discharged, we experience pleasure. Tensions may originate from within or from without, but what is important is that we are homeostatic systems, fundamentally trying to regulate the tensions that we experience. According to Freud, we relate to others because they can serve to help us relieve our tensions and thus give us pleasure.

Since we are studying Freud, after all, we should use the example of sex. In this view, sexual desire is a tension that we experience from within, due to body impulses and thoughts, or from without, due to various instinctually and culturally determined signals. In seeking to discharge this tension, we may relate to others because of their ability to help us relieve our tensions and provide us with pleasure.

Theorists subsequent to Freud wrestled with the problem of how and why human beings are motivated to act as they do, and how other human beings figure into the equation. Most vital, these theorists began to study children and infants; this makes complete sense, since Freud himself was the one who postulated the importance of early childhood development. Freud, however, did little clinical observation and work with children, and it was left to his daughter, Anna Freud, Erik Erikson, and many others to study human development at the source.

In essence, psychoanalytic theory and practice moved toward a deep and abiding concern with the development of the infant and child in the context of the care-taking relationship. As Greenberg and Mitchell (1983) say, Fairbairn and other psychoanalytic theorists suggest that babies are oriented toward other people from birth and that this propensity to relate to others is not accidental, but serves important adaptive purposes and is crucially related to who we are as human beings. Our relationships with others, first with our primary caretaker, then with all the other people in our lives, are of primary importance and fundamentally shaped our personalities, for good and for ill. Because these relationships are so important, therapeutic treatment must also be centrally preoccupied with a client's early and subsequent relationships.

Self

Following treatments such as Pine (1990) and textbooks (e.g., Sharf, 2012), we discuss the self separately, though again as with the Ego, there is much continuity with the other categories, especially with object relations. Self psychology is primarily associated with Kohut (1971) and his work on the treatment of narcissistic personality disorders. Kohut describes the development of self and object for normalcy and for narcissistic personality disorders and psychoses. To develop normally in Kohut's view, "the self develops out of certain key relationships, which he terms self-object relationships, in which the parents serve not just as objects of the child's needs and desires, but as providers of certain 'narcissistic' functions...in which the child is seen as perfect by the admiring parent or the parent is seen as perfect and linked to an admiring child" (Mitchell, 1988, p. 32).

Kohut (1971) interestingly locates the development of the experience of both self and other on a continuum, from psychosis at the lowest functioning, through narcissistic personality disorders, to normalcy. At the lowest level, the self is experienced in a psychotic fashion—as a kind of adult version of the childhood grandiosity of self, in which the child pretends to be

King of the Universe. Frequently in clinical settings, schizophrenic individuals express this kind of grandiosity, imagining that they are Jesus or another great figure from the past. At the next level, that of ongoing narcissism, there are what Kohut terms "solipsistic claims for attention" (p. 9), in which the person fundamentally believes himself to be performing on a stage with one character—himself. At the highest level, that of normalcy, there is a "mature form of positive self-esteem; self-confidence" (p. 9).

Similarly, the person's experience of others occurs on a continuum. At the level of psychosis, the person experiences "delusional reconstitution of the omnipotent object; the powerful persecutor, the influencing machine" (Kohut, 1971, p. 9). In clinical settings, it is strikingly common for individuals with schizophrenia to speak of an omnipotent agency (such as the case of the young man who referred to The Man with palpable dread) that is pursuing them mercilessly. At the level of narcissistic personality disorders, there is a "compelling need for merger with powerful object" (p. 9) which can be over-idealized and thus venerated, but also deeply disappointing and worthy of contempt. At the level of normalcy, there is "mature form of admiration for others; ability for enthusiasm" (p. 9).

Kohut (1971) says that in "a successfully lived, paradigmatic life" there is a "progression from information through knowledge to wisdom" (p. 326) that can be seen in successful treatment: "As the treatment begins, analyst and analysand are gathering *information* about the patient and his history. Gradually, in the middle phases of the analysis, the data which have been collected become ordered and fitted together into a broader and deeper *knowledge* of the cohesive functioning of the patient's mind and of the continuity which exists between the present and the past. And, finally, in the termination phase of a good analysis, the analyst's knowledge and the patient's understanding of himself have taken on the quality of *wisdom*. In order to reach this experience, the patient must first have come to terms with his unmodified infantile narcissism, whether his fixations were predominately on the archaic grandiose self or on the archaic, narcissistic aggrandized, idealized self object" (pp. 326–327). In this passage, Kohut gives a useful summary not only of his particular form of analysis, but also one that could characterize all successful forms of therapeutic treatment. Kohut says that we must successfully develop beyond the fundamentally narcissistic self of the infant and the idealized (and confusing) self-object. We need to develop a healthy self-esteem that integrates a recognition of both our strengths and our own limitations, as well as a healthy respect and esteem for others without falling into the error of overly idealizing them or mercilessly denigrating them.

Quick Clinical Vignettes

Drive, Ego, Object Relations, and Self

Drive—Thomas was sexually attracted to young girls. He was diagnosed with paranoid schizophrenia and major depression and had a past history of drug and alcohol abuse. His was an example of someone who struggled with thoughts and urges that go against fundamental societal norms. Due to his schizophrenia, he also struggled with how to battle these urges. He struggled with being reality based; his rational thinking had been battered by years of drug abuse and by persistent and intrusive thoughts. Moreover, these intrusive thoughts were horribly critical and vicious, telling him that he was worthless and deserved to die. Thus Thomas's rational capabilities (Ego) had to contend with his overwhelming attraction to young girls (Id), the harshly critical voices he heard in his head (Superego), and the realistic demands of society.

Ego—Operations of the Ego can be harder to pinpoint, because they can appear simply as normal and healthy responses, and thus invisible. One of the most clear clinical examples was furnished by the above individual, Thomas. Despite his struggles with schizophrenia, despite his depression, despite his awareness that if people knew of his pedophilia they would despise him (and perhaps want to physically hurt him) he was the hardest-working client I have ever encountered. He regularly attended individual and group therapy and faithfully did his homework. When he was out on trips with residential staff, he would alert them whenever he experienced sexual urges as a result of seeing a girl and asked them to escort him back to the van. To combat the sexual thoughts and urges that he felt when he saw young girls, he would smell and taste a cotton strip soaked in a solution of concentrated goldenseal, a very bitter herb. This client practiced this very aversive therapy to train himself out of his sexual desire for young children—an amazing example of the power of the heroic Ego.

Object relations—From the perspective of object relations, the counselor needs to be a good object—that is, the counselor needs to provide "opportunities for relatedness hitherto unavailable to or unutilizable by the patient" (Mitchell, 1988, p. 152), new opportunities that weren't available in the primary caretaking relationships that the person experienced. Interestingly, we often know what it is like to be a good object through being a bad object. This was illustrated to me most clearly not in a relationship with a client, but with a counseling supervisee. At one point, our agency was audited; as the clinic director, I was responsible to make sure the client files were in order. Noticing this supervisee had several files that were lacking, and knowing that she wouldn't be in for several days, I went into her desk, pulled the information to complete the files, and left her a message that told her what I had done.

The supervisee called me back and said, with barely contained rage, "You violated my rights! You violated me!"

Internally, I felt like I had done something terribly wrong—even though I knew that I had done nothing wrong. After we hung up, the supervisee's attacks rang in my ears—"You violated me!" Hoping to get some perspective, I spoke to a fellow clinic director in our agency; my colleague knew the supervisee

(Continued)

(Continued)

quite well (she worked at his site as well as mine), and after listening to me he said, "You were the bad object."

Instantly I understood—my colleague had given me a framework that told me that I had participated in a very deep and important struggle with this supervisee, in which she treated me as a bad object from her past. With this knowledge, I worked to regain my equilibrium and become the good object again.

Self—In working with a client named Stephen, my aim was to help him gain a healthy self- and other esteem. He tended to oscillate between contempt for himself ("I'm such an idiot! I need a complete personality overhaul!") and a solipsistic focus on himself. He also oscillated between over-idealizing people (myself included) as well as contempt for them when they failed him (myself included).

Stephen said that he felt like he was trying to grow a new shell. The metaphor of molting a shell is an apt one. A client can feel like he has lost his shell and is intensely vulnerable to the world; but this is entirely necessary, because the old shell was too small, and to grow, he needs to shed his old shell—his defenses and way of dealing with the world—to grow a new, larger shell that will accommodate his larger self. But the time of molting is one of intense vulnerability, and the creature—soft, vulnerable, unprotected—may react blindly and with terror to its surroundings if it perceives a threat.

So did it seem with Stephen. In working with him, I continually had the feeling that he could fall apart at any second, especially if I said anything remotely challenging to him—yet he hung on.

Over the space of several years, his sense of self solidified, and his relationships with others steadied; and after termination, he seemed to have a snug shell—he had grown his own home.

Neuroscience and Psychoanalysis

As we recall, one of the enduring themes inaugurated by Freud was the investigation into the causes of mental illness and the apparent either/or nature of the problem—the cause of mental illness was either psychological or it was biological. But we also remember that this is a false dichotomy. Modern commentators remind us that Freud "who was best known for his original and perceptive insights into the psychology of mental illness, in fact maintained a consistent interest in biology" (Ostow, 2004, p. xv), and we must keep in mind that modern biological psychiatry have returned to Freud's contributions to this topic and have shown an interest in reintegrating his theory with important findings from contemporary neuroscience. Turnbull and Solms (2004) revisit the varieties of psychiatric changes following brain injury and disease by reexamining Freud's depth psychology, bringing "the observational techniques of psychoanalysis to bear on matters of prime concern to cognitive neuroscience" (p. 573). In their research, they discuss the explanatory power of Freud's concept of the unconscious and apply it to patients suffering from brain injury. They argue that Freud's concepts of the unconscious "throw important light on a number of syndromes that neurocognitive theories cannot fully explain" (p. 590) and suggest that targeted therapies based on psychoanalytic principles can be developed to address these psychiatric syndromes.

This new synthesis is taken up by others as well. Updating Freudian terms, Kaplan (2004) suggests that "what Freud called *instinctual drives* can be described in modern terms as the basic emotional operating systems that are mediated by subcortical structures" (p. 549) and goes on to say that "psychoanalysis has always had as its goal the sculpting of subcortico-cortical functions via the relationships between analyst and patient" (pp. 549–550). What this means, in plain English, is that contemporary researchers have come to think that counseling (in this case, psychoanalysis) can change brain functioning and affective experience in biological, structural, system-wide ways (we examine this in greater detail when we discuss Schore's [1994, 2003, 2011] contributions).

On the theme of psychotropic medication, we find that Kaplan (2004) argues for combining psychoanalytic treatment with medication, suggesting that while "medication restores basic functions such as sleep, appetite, concentration, and energy, stabilizes mood, and relieves anxiety or psychosis," it "does not address the underlying etiology of that turmoil" (p. 557). Significantly, medications may have broad, general impacts, but they are "distressingly nonspecific in their capacity to manipulate psychological processes, even as we come to understand these processes at neurochemical and neurophysiological levels" (p. 566). These ideas are quite consistent with contemporary clinical practice. We still do not know how psychotropic medication works, and the consensus about the interaction of medication and psychotherapeutic treatment is roughly consistent with Kaplan's position—medication appears to often have some broad positive impact, and counseling appears to provide the individualized plan for specific positive change.

The Development of the Emotional Self

Schore's (1994, 2003, 2011) work has been central to this intersection of contemporary brain research and psychoanalytic clinical practice, in particular how psychoanalysis may be involved in refashioning subcortical functions in the therapeutic relationship between clinician and client. In his many publications, he makes the same essential points over and over again. First, given the research on left brain and right brain development, he suggests that "the early developing right brain generates the implicit self, the structural system of the human consciousness" (Schore, 2011, p. 75). That is, in the context of early relational experiences, the right brain organizes, at a less-than-conscious level, the emotional experiences of the developing individual. This involves frontal, midbrain, and hindbrain sectors of the brain, in which the most primitive part of the brain—the hindbrain—is modulated by midbrain—and finally frontal and prefrontal cortices.

For those of us who are nonscientists, the best way to understand it is through the equation of hindbrain operations as reptilian response, midbrain as mammalian responses, and finally the frontal and prefrontal responses as the uniquely human responses. It is important to realize that humans experience emotions like crocodiles (hindbrain) and like mice and tigers (midbrain); we also have the unimaginably complex emotional responses like ennui (an indefinable kind of melancholy and sadness) and schadenfreude (taking pleasure in the misfortunes of others), both of which appear to be qualitatively different than anything that even the most intelligent of mammals experience (forebrain).

Second, one of this implicit self's primary tasks is to develop the ability to effectively regulate emotional states, modulating negative affective states and enhancing and sustaining positive affective states. Since we experience powerful instinctual responses as well as highly sophisticated, cognitively mediated impressions and reminiscences, the implicit self must develop effective strategies to process emotional responses that range from overwhelming to barely discernible.

Third, successful regulation cannot, in this view, be developed by the individual, but must be developed in the context of interpersonal relationships. Schore (2011) builds on object relations and attachment theory to show how the implicit self is fostered in intense, less-than-conscious interpersonal interactions. As he puts it, "during spontaneous right brain-to-right brain visual-facial, auditory, prosodic, and tactile proprioceptive emotionally charged attachment communications, the sensitive, psychobiologically attuned caregiver regulates, at an implicit level, the infant's states of arousal" (p. 79).

NEUROSCIENCE OF THE DEVELOPMENT OF EMOTIONS, SIMPLIFIED

- We initially experience emotions in primitive, less-differentiated ways; as time goes on, we still experience emotion in primitive ways, but also in increasingly more sophisticated, patterned, and systematic ways, including increasing awareness of emotions themselves.
- Research suggests that our right forebrain organizes midbrain (mammalian) and hindbrain (reptilian) responses.

- Schore (1994, 2003, 2011) suggests that an implicit self arises that structures our consciousness.
- A primary task of our implicit self is to effectively regulate emotional states by (1) dampening negative states and (2) enhancing and sustaining positive states. In other words, we must figure out how to stop being in sad or depressed moods, and learn how to get into happy and content moods—and stay in them.
- We develop or fail to develop the ability to accomplish this task in the context of interpersonal relationships.
- Caregivers and significant figures in our infancy and childhood need to help us. At first, when we are in infancy, they must do most of the work. They need to recognize when we are sad or hungry, when we need attention, food, or to be changed, and so on, and employ caretaking behaviors to make us feel better—feed us, sing to us, distract us, help us go to sleep, and so forth. They also need to recognize when we are happy and help us stay in that groove.
- As we develop, they need to teach us how to recognize our emotional states and to employ creative strategies to accomplish the two fundamental tasks of emotional self-regulation. Less-than-helpful responses from caregivers: "Stop crying and act like a big girl!" "Stop your sniveling or I'll really give you something to cry about!" "Stop being so emotional!" More helpful responses: "You seem sad. Do you want to talk about it?" "Losing a family pet can be really hard. I'm sad too. Let's go out to the playground and have some fun, and we can talk about it later when we are both feeling a little better, okay?"
- As we continue to develop, they need to fade their own involvement, while still supporting our attempts to meet our own needs. As we mature, they need to continue to offer support and encouragement. Throughout this process, Vygotsky's (1978) idea of the zone of proximal development is relevant here—learning occurs at the place where what-I-can-do-by-myself meets what-I-can-do-with-the-help-of-others.
- Failure to develop the ability to emotionally self-regulate may cause significant problems for us, including depression, anxiety, drug and alcohol use, and dysfunctional and dissatisfying interpersonal relationships. The idea is that our responses to problems often create more and more lasting problems for us than the original problem (Watzlawick, Weakland, & Fisch, 1974) and that these responses are often based on our emotional reactivity.
- Counseling offers the opportunity to reeducate clients in more functional emotional responses. The counselor attunes herself, at both conscious and unconscious levels, to the patterns of emotional arousal experienced by her clients. She helps identify functional response patterns and broaden and generalize these responses. She helps identify, extinguish, and replace other less-functional response patterns, and/or decrease the frequency of particular response patterns and diversify them.

An Illustration: Daddy Day Care

Picture the following scene: a mother, who is going stir-crazy, goes out for a latte with her girlfriends, leaving dad in charge of their baby girl.

Dad is crazy in love with this little creature, and when mom leaves, he sweeps her up in the way that baby loves (and that causes a heart attack in baby's mother) and slowly dances around the house with his daughter in his arms. Baby squeals with delight, dad hums and looks deeply into his daughter's eyes, and they share a moment of unblinking connection. Then baby starts to seem a little alarmed, and dad, knowing that this means that their contact has become a little too intense, slows his dancing and looks away, giving his daughter time to regain her equilibrium. When he senses that she is ready again, he looks back and her and raises his eyebrows, which provokes a delighted expression on her face. They continue dancing together in this way for the entire afternoon; dad regulating their experience together, being sensitive to his daughter's needs to come together and to rest apart, to feed, digest, sleep, and awake and interact.

In doing so, he is not just dealing with his child's physical needs, but he is also helping the baby learn how to deal with sad states and how to experience happy states. At first, when the baby is tiny, she has a very, very limited ability to self-regulate, and he functions, as it were, as an external regulator, smiling to get the baby to smile, laughing to help her laugh, making concerned expressions when the baby is crying, and in general trying to anticipate future emotional states and to improve current ones. As the infant grows into a toddler, then into a young child and beyond, he will gradually fade his role and allow his developing daughter to take over more and more of the regulation duties.

With this ideal development in mind, it then follows that early childhood trauma—neglectful or abusive experiences, or at a less extreme level, inattentive or unskillful parenting—tends to impair the ability to successfully regulate emotion, in effect impairing the development of the implicit self that Schore (2011) describes. In the above example, dad is attuned and skillful; if the adult is not attuned, is unskillful, uncaring, or is actually abusive or neglectful, the child is given woefully insufficient training in how to modulate complex emotional reactions. As Schore (2011) says, "in contrast to an optimal attachment scenario, in a relational growth-inhibiting early environment the primary caregiver of an insecure disorganized disoriented infant induces traumatic states of enduring negative affect in the child" (p. 80). The child is insecure—because it cannot figure out how to process and interpret the many conflicting signals in its environment. The child is disorganized, because it is not given any helpful guidelines about how to react. The child is disoriented, because there appears to be no solid footing—everything seems to happen and change at the same time.

Counseling as a Corrective Affective (and Cognitive) Experience

Counseling can provide a corrective affective experience for the client—"in an optimal context the empathic therapist can potentially act as implicit regulator of the patient's conscious and dissociated unconscious affective states. This dyadic psychobiological corrective emotional experience can lead to the emergence of more complex psychic structure by increasing the connectivity of right brain limbic-autonomic circuits" (Schore, 2011, p. 84). Again in plain English, the counselor can in effect help reparent the client, helping the client develop more functional regulation of emotions. In Schore's view, this help occurs primarily at a nonconscious level. He describes it this way: "The intuitive psychobiologically attuned therapist, on a moment-to-moment basis, implicitly focuses her countertransferential broad attentional processes upon patterns of rhythmic crescendos/decrescendos of the patient's regulated and dysregulated states of affective autonomic arousal" and "must both remain psychobiologically attuned to the patient in a state of right brain evenly suspended attention and at the same time access an intuitive fast, emotional, and effortless right brain decision process to navigate through the stressful intersubjective context" (Schore, 2011, p. 89).

What this means is that the counselor's right brain must be in close connection with the client's right brain, just as the caregiver's fully developed right brain is in close connection with the developing infant's. In this close connection, untold connections and reactions occur, most at an unconscious level, and patterns of arousal and regulation are learned; it is Schore's belief that a primary use of counseling and psychotherapy is to witness the reenactment of past dysfunctional patterns of emotional regulation and to replace these dysfunctional patterns with more functional ones.

We should also remember that though we have been primarily describing affect—feelings—our inquiry is inextricably involved with cognitions—thoughts. Though there has been a longstanding Western tradition of opposing feelings and thoughts, modern brain researchers increasingly recognize that thoughts and feelings are not opposed and that to separate them into two distinct categories is an error that has been persistent throughout Western philosophical traditions (Damasio, 1994). Instead, modern researchers say that "cognition would be rudderless without the accompaniment of emotion, just as emotion would be primitive without the participation of cognition" (Davidson, 2000, p. 91). We should remember that it is equally important to pay attention to feelings that arise in treatment—through our affective attunement with clients—and help clients modulate these feelings and make them more adaptive, as well as to help clients use their cognitive, critical reasoning skills to address life's complex tasks. Doesn't this sound familiar? It should, because Freud said it first.

Summary

- In considering the many updates of Freud's theory, we can most usefully characterize them as doing two things:

    1. Turning our focus from a purely internal, one-person model to a relational, two-person model
    2. Integrating neuroscientific findings into clinical theory and practice

- Traditionally, four schools have been identified—Freud's original drive theory, Ego psychology, Object Relations, and self psychology.

    1. Originally, Freud described the ongoing conflict within an individual, and located various stages at which development can become arrested (e.g., Oral/Anal/Phallic).
    2. In Ego psychology, the concern remains with the fundamental integrity of the Ego and its ability to serve a harmonizing and mediating role in the conflict originally described by Freud.
    3. In Object Relations, there is an ever-increasing focus on the development of the individual in the context of primary human relationships.
    4. In self psychology, the focus is on fully and accurately experiencing one's self as self, and objects as objects; we must fully see ourselves and fully see others, owning our strengths and weaknesses and being able to like and esteem others, even though they may disappoint us.

- Neuroscience can helpfully update Freud's project. Indeed, long-term analytic treatment can be described as having as its goal the resculpting of cortical functions—to actually change brain structure and functioning, which finds support in contemporary brain research.
- While psychopharmacological treatment continues to burgeon, serious critiques attend the use of medication, including the presence of serious side effects for some; counseling continues to provide an individualized treatment plan for psychological distress.
- Schore suggests that we develop an implicit emotional self to accomplish two fundamental tasks:

    1. To dampen negative affect (sadness, worry, etc.)
    2. To enhance and sustain positive affect (joy, interest, etc.)

- Counseling can provide a powerful, corrective affective—and cognitive—experience.

4

Multiculturalism

In this chapter, we examine the sociocultural context of psychoanalysis. In doing so, we concentrate our efforts on three multicultural contexts that have greatly impacted and continue to impact psychoanalysis and all subsequent counseling: race/ethnicity, social class and gender. These three contexts, which can be described in terms of group belonging or group affiliation (Hollinger, 1995), are an essential part of the evolution that was described in the preceding chapter. As we examine these contexts, we complete our understanding not only of the development of psychoanalysis, but also of the clients whom we serve, and in so doing prepare to look at the extended clinical example in the next chapter. Remember that from a common factors perspective, the focus should always remain on the client; to fundamentally understand our clients, we must pay attention to the multilayered contexts in which they find themselves.

"My Parents Were Jews, and I Have Remained a Jew Myself"

The leitmotif to Freud's life and career was his status as a Jew in anti-Semitic Europe. As Gay (2006) amply documents, the Austria that Freud grew up in was a contradiction; it held within it both a liberal and relatively benign attitude toward religious and social minorities as well as hidden and overt racist attitudes. Throughout Freud's life, there was an ongoing tension between these polarities, between a spirit of openness that allowed Freud to dream of being fully recognized in academic and professional spheres and a spirit of intolerance and racial hatred that produced racially tinged critiques of his work. Freud lived and worked in a rising tide of fascism and racial intolerance that was more than simply the product of a few crazed individuals but in fact permeated European society.

It is important to remember that the Holocaust was not simply the creation of the Nazis, of an evil few who coerced an unwilling population into committing horrific acts; there has been a compelling line of research that demonstrates that ordinary Germans willingly and often enthusiastically participated in the murder of Jews (Browning, 1992; Goldhagen, 1996). This is actually very much in line with Freud: remember that in Freud's view, it's not just the Hitlers of the world who have an Id—we all have murderous aggression. In Vienna, where Freud lived from an early age and where he worked for his entire professional life, there was a degree of public and professional acceptance for Jews, but Freud confronted anti-Semitism throughout his career. Racism was an indelible part of his experience growing up (his lifelong ambivalence about his own father was partially caused by Freud's feelings of shame at what he perceived to be his father's meek submission to racism), continued throughout his career, and haunted his last days. At the end of his life, he and his immediate family were able to leave Austria after the Anschluss (the invasion of Austria by Germany), but his sisters were murdered in the Holocaust.

It is important to read Freud's work within this historical context. Freud was concerned with developing a psychological theory that was broadly applicable, and he was always a bit defensive that it would be seen as a "Jewish theory." In the extreme, some writers who identified as Christians thought that Freud was merely exposing what had been known all along—that Jews were degenerate, sensual, and less-than-human; Christians, they thought, weren't made like that. It is important to acknowledge that noxious sentiments like this were the context for the development of Freud's theory. He was constantly explaining what psychoanalysis was, and if one reads his work closely, one is struck by how he continually reassures his reader. If we again use Freud's own methods here, we would be very interested in what was unconsciously motivating Freud; one could argue that his urbane and sophisticated writing persona was aimed at calming anxieties that might arise in the reader, anxieties that were likely tinged with racial fears.

Social Class: Is Psychoanalysis Just for Rich People?

It is thus ironic that Freud, who considered himself an outsider (Gay, 1989b) and was marginalized as a Jew in a Christian country, came to be identified with a clinical practice that was and is regarded as elitist and even potentially discriminatory against diverse populations. Put simply, many people believed and still believe that psychoanalysis is only for rich people. The argument goes that it is too expensive on the one hand for any but the wealthiest clientele, and on the other that its methods require that the client have the ability and interest to engage in deep self-examination and personal insight—activities that only the middle and upper classes are able to engage in. There are two ways to approach this problem—one that focuses on practical concerns, the other on theoretical. Let's first tackle the practical issues.

Practical Matters First: Money

Heading the list of practical concerns is indeed money. Freud often dismissed the United States as being obsessed with the almighty dollar, but he was himself always concerned with financial security. It is not hard to understand why. To read his financial preoccupations in light of his biography is another very Freudian activity, and Freud's childhood was beset with financial worries—his father and his extended family suffered a series of financial setbacks, and though Freud was given adequate resources to pursue his studies (he was given his own room, while his sisters had to share, for example), he grew up in an atmosphere of financial insecurity.

When Freud married and began a family, his first pragmatic priority was to establish an upper-middle-class household that was not marred by material want. And as a doctor who was attempting to establish a new practice—new in the sense of attracting new patients, and new in the sense of inaugurating an entirely new specialty area—he needed to see people who could afford it: "the necessities of our existence limit our work to the well-to-do classes, who are accustomed to choose their own physicians" (Freud, 1919/1955, p. 166). This class of people had the educational resources that might help them be receptive to a new treatment method and the financial resources to pay for it.

A Theoretical Concern: Who Has Time for Insight?

And interestingly enough, this practical and pragmatic issue hints at the second issue, that of theory. One argument goes that only the middle and upper classes have the time for a full examination of their mental life; the poor are too preoccupied by material deprivation to do so; since they are so consumed with the practical aspects of their lives, they have no time to reflect on the life of their minds. This is a "charitable" way of putting it;

there have been more pernicious expressions of this idea, which says that the poor are less intelligent and constitutionally unable to be reflective.

Even if one adopts a more charitable view—that if you are poor, you don't really have time to be neurotic, whereas if you are rich, you have time to reflect on your life, and to worry about it and work yourself into a neurosis—one is faced with a problem, from an analytic point of view. As we know by now, the central aim of psychoanalysis is to bring unconscious material into conscious awareness, and to strengthen the Ego so that rather than overusing defense mechanisms that are inadequate to the task of dealing with life in all its complexity, the Ego is able to face the issues that once seemed so overwhelming and now make calm, mature, rational decisions about them (Freud, 1926/2002). This presupposes a great deal of insight—a person must become aware of this repressed material and have the capacity to understand how their habitual responses really just aren't up for the task. (This is seen in modern times in the Dr. Phil question—when he interviews a person stuck in a self-defeating pattern who nonetheless seems reluctant to give up this pattern, Dr. Phil asks them, "How's that working for you?" knowing full well that the honest answer is, "Not so well.")

One doesn't need to adopt an extreme position in terms of the need for leisure in order to be reflective to recognize a conundrum here. People across the spectrum of financial concerns—from those who worry about getting enough to eat and having a roof over one's head to those who worry about making a mortgage or car payment to those who worry about having the money to send their children to elite institutions and even those who worry about where to park their third or fourth or fifth car—can identify that these concerns make it hard to focus on more abstract questions. If one's stomach is grumbling, it's hard to think. And psychoanalysis asks people to think, and think hard about their lives.

Theoretical Concern Number Two: Who Has the Necessary Ego Strength?

A second theoretical issue is the idea that it requires a certain degree of ego strength to tolerate a classical analysis. As we recall, Freud (1919/1955) said that "it was a frustration that made the patient ill, and that his symptoms serve him as substitutive satisfactions" (pp. 162–163). Life consists of many internal and external struggles, and if the Ego is insufficient to the task, it tends to flee from these struggles. It may deny that these struggles exist, locate an internal struggle in the external world, or mismanage a response in other ways. Rather than developing a mature and resilient Ego that can tolerate frustration and face anxiety, people tend to engage in all sorts of childish responses. They blame others when it's clear that their actions have produced an undesirable situation. They engage in behavior that is clearly self-defeating and bewildering to those around them. In modern parlance, neurosis develops when people take the easy way out—but as people find out to their dismay, the easy way out in fact can create hardship and misery.

Freud said people will try to take the easy way out in treatment as well. Again, he warned that many patients will be satisfied with halfway measures and partial cures; he also recognized that clinicians will want to go easy on their patients out of sympathy for them. But "in so doing they make no attempt to give him more strength for facing life and more capacity for carrying out his actual tasks in it" (Freud, 1919/1955, p. 164). Rather, the clinician must maintain a great deal of reserve and avoid an easy gratification of a patient's wishes—"as far as his relations with the physician are concerned, the patient must be left with unfulfilled wishes in abundance" (p. 164).

When the analyst remains objective and detached, he serves as a blank screen upon which the patient's past and present anxieties and defense mechanisms show up most clearly. To continue the cinematic metaphor, if an analyst satisfies the patient's wishes, it would be as if the blank screen would begin playing its own movie, and the movie projected onto the screen by the patient would be hopelessly confused with it.

People who lack material resources are, by definition, needy—they need access to healthcare, to education, to jobs. And if they come in for treatment, even treatment that is by definition mental and psychological rather than material and economic, these needs will invariably surface in treatment. From a classical point of view, the clinician must not respond to these practical needs, because to do so would muddy the waters. What is important, from the classical viewpoint, is that the patient begin to express the deeper, underlying psychological needs that may be expressed on the surface as material needs. The transference relationship revolves around these deep wishes; the analyst's job is to figure out what these wishes represent, not to quickly satisfy them.

Thus, from this classical perspective, the analyst may be in the unhappy position of telling the poor patient, in effect, "Look, I know that your heat is about to be shut off, and I know that you want me to help you brainstorm about how to come up with ideas to prevent this, but I wonder if you could instead tell me about whether this situation reminds you of other periods of deprivation in your life—remember that you told once that you felt your mother never really gave you the nurturing that you needed?" While this may seem ridiculous to the modern reader, it does appear to flow inexorably from a classical point of view.

The Relational Response

Fortunately, there is another analytic perspective that furnishes both a theoretical and practical response, that of relational psychoanalysis (Greenberg & Mitchell, 1983). This view says that the therapeutic relationship itself furnishes both the "stuff" that can and should be analyzed as well as opportunity for the client to practice new and more functional ways of relating. From a relational perspective, everything that a client brings into counseling, and everything that the clinician brings, furnishes wonderful, real-time opportunities to examine dysfunctional and functional ways of relating to self, others, and the larger world. In this view, a discussion about the possibility of having one's heat shut off is an opportunity to explore practical avenues to address this, as well as examining whether this is a typical pattern for the client, the implications of using counseling time on brainstorming solutions, how the counseling relationship might be strengthened by such help, and how it might be weakened if solutions are not found or, if found, are discovered to be transitory.

And most important for our present discussion, these conversations must include culture as the shaping context for our material and psychological needs, wants, desires, and wishes. As Altman (2010) suggests, psychoanalytic theorists have historically "ignored class, culture, and race as powerful elements in the psychoanalytic field only by being unreflectively embedded in our society's arrangements with regard to these categories" (p. xviii). Fortunately, as psychoanalysis took a turn toward the relational, it also took a turn toward being more reflective of the impact of diverse group affiliations such as race, culture, gender, and class. There have been important recent psychoanalytic developments in Asia (Gerlach, Hooke, & Varvin, 2013) that have helped identify and formulate key concerns on the part of West, which is concerned about maintaining the essential aspects of psychoanalysis, and the East, which is concerned with maintaining Asian culture and outlooks in the practice and theory of psychoanalysis (Hooke, Varvin, & Gerlach, 2013). There has been concerted recent efforts to look at psychoanalytic and psychodynamic treatment through the prisms of race, culture, and class (e.g., Gelman, 2003; Javier & Herron, 2002; Leary, 2012), treatments that include cultural and linguistic critiques as well (e.g., Lane, 1998).

In addition, Altman (2010) provides what is perhaps the best practical and theoretical response to the charges of elitism in psychoanalysis in his wonderful account of his years spent in practice in the Bronx, *An Analyst in the Inner City: Race, Class and Culture Through a Psychoanalytic Lens.* These contemporary accounts furnish a counter-narrative to the common perception of psychoanalysis as elitist. While there is a considerable need for empirical psychoanalytic and psychodynamic research on diverse populations (Watkins, 2012, 2013), researchers and clinicians are grappling with how to make Freud useful for contemporary counselors in their work with diverse populations, which is the central preoccupation of this book as well.

Quick Clinical Vignette

It's Not Always What You Think—The Importance of Group Salience

Approaching clients from a multicultural perspective, we need to continue to look to the clients for information on how we can best understand the groups that they belong to and their allegiance to these groups. The idea that people demonstrate varying degrees of allegiance to groups, and that this allegiance varies across time and settings, is called *salience*. Think about yourself—if you are presently a graduate student, you might consider this to be a primary identifying characteristic, perhaps even trumping other important group memberships such as culture and gender. And how important this membership is to you depends on setting (relatively more important when you are with other graduate students, for example) as well as chronology (this membership was not important to you before you became a graduate student, and will become much less important to you after you graduate).

This is an important concept to keep in mind when working with clients and was illustrated by a client I saw. She was in her early thirties, and as I thought about my work with her, I considered that it might be important to address with her the fact that she was a Latina in a small, overwhelmingly white (80% white, and 20% very white, as the joke goes) community in rural Iowa.

This turned out to be somewhat important to her—but her most important group affiliation was far different. In her conversation with me, she referred to her partner as *Master*. I followed up with questions about this term, and we were soon discussing her membership in a group I knew nothing about, which was a consensual BDSM (bondage and discipline, dominance and submission, sadism and masochism) community (see Yost & Hunter, 2012, for a scholarly account of how BDSM community members construct their identities). In her eyes, her relationship and her identity was primarily found in this group affiliation. The takeaway in this case was that even well-meaning assumptions about the salience of a client's group memberships can be substantially in error—and that yet again, we must inquire into the clients' experience and follow their lead.

Recent Scholarship: The Free Clinics

Before moving on to another crucial group affiliation, gender, it is important to note that recent scholarship has found that this preoccupation with making psychoanalytic treatment relevant to underresourced populations is in fact not a modern phenomenon. Danto's (2005) fascinating book,

Freud's Free Clinics: Psychoanalysis & Social Justice, 1918–1938, shows that Freud and his followers were well aware of the elitist nature of their enterprise and took concrete steps to address this problem.

Freud, though he was always concerned with making a living and supporting his family, was a charitable man in both theory and practice. While he originally thought it was important to charge a fee that demonstrated the value of treatment—"it is well known that you do not make the patient value a treatment more by underselling it" (Freud, 1913/2002, p. 53)—he came to realize that psychoanalysis was not reaching populations that deserved help, and "until the end of his life Freud supported free psychoanalytic clinics, stood up for the flexible fee, and defended the practice of lay analysis" (Danto, 2005, p. 13).

Between the years of 1918 and 1938, at least 13 cooperative psychoanalytic mental health clinics were established, where students and established practitioners donated their time so that people with limited resources could be treated. Freud himself donated time to free treatment ("for about ten years I gave free consultations for an hour a day, sometimes two," Freud, 1913/2002, p. 53) and endorsed vouchers that could be redeemed at Vienna's free treatment center, the Ambulatorium (Danto, 2005). While the rise to power of the Nazis and World War II put an end to these charitable activities in 1938, it is important to note that psychoanalysis possessed a strong social consciousness from its beginnings, a social consciousness that was somewhat lost in the United States until more recent developments revived it (e.g., Altman, 2010).

Psychoanalysis as Failed Feminism

According to a feminist critique, psychoanalysis mystifies women's experience; famously, Freud once asked, "Was will das Weib"—What does a woman want? (or more colloquially, What do women want?). Implicit in this question is an attitude that women are difficult to figure out, unpredictable, unknown. In asking this question, Freud implies that women are somehow mysteriously motivated and that what women want is fundamentally different than what men want. That is precisely the problem, according to a feminist critique. To ask the question, *What do women want?* implies that what men want and what women want are somehow distinct. But contrary to standup comics and misguided tomes that attempt to explain the fundamental differences between men and women (Men are from Mars! Women are from Venus!), women and men want the same basic things—to have their bodily needs met, to have their social needs met, to be able to laugh, think, feel, and to have the freedom to fully express their humanity and the full range of experiences as a human being.

Are Men and Women Really Different?

Certainly, there may be some socialized differences. But in a strange turnaround, it seems as if the burden of proof rests on the person who says, "Women and men are fundamentally the same" rather than on the person who says, "Women and men are fundamentally different." When I raise gender issues in class, many women and many men identify profound differences between men and women. We often have a great time outlining these differences and laughing about them. There is a sense that life would be much poorer without these wonderful (and sometimes wonderfully erotic) differences between male and female. It is important to acknowledge that these differences, even if they are mostly likely highly socialized differences, can be a source of fun and erotic delight.

But it is also clear that the accumulated weight of millennia of socialized misogyny hasn't done women, or any men who care about fairness, justice, and equality, any favors. As late as 2011, women who worked full time earned 82% of the mean earnings of men who worked full time (United States Bureau of Labor Statistics, 2012), and there is no indication that the "second shift" phenomenon—where women come home from working to take over the majority of the childcare and housework—is a thing of the past (Hochschild & Machung, 2012). Where there are differences between men and women, it usually is the case that the difference puts women at a disadvantage.

Empirical Research to the Rescue

And we do need to be carefully examining the gender differences that have been put forth. Hyde (2005), in her meta-analysis of supposed psychological and physical differences, found only a few significant ones: throwing, both distance and velocity and certain other aspects of physical performance. But it is important to note that within group differences are great—for example, Serena and Venus Williams in tennis, who serve faster than most men in the world (including men in the professional tennis circuit), and Brittney Griner, who could dunk the basketball on most men in the world. There were a few other differences. In sexuality, there was a huge discrepancy for rates of masturbation (unsurprisingly, men reported doing it a lot more than women), and attitudes about sex in a casual, uncommitted relationship (men were decidedly for it, women were less enthusiastic). Regarding aggression—men tended to be more physically aggressive, but women may be equal or greater in relational aggression.

But other than that, there were no meaningfully significant differences between men and women—and this in a world in which vast energy is expended on making men and women different! Think about it—what is usually the first question when a child is born? Is it, *Is it healthy?* Is it, *How do you feel about being parents?* Or is it, *Is it a boy or a girl?* Think about how vital it seems to parents to enforce gender differences, down to the color of clothing and room. Even forward-thinking men and women find themselves giving in to the gender police and discourage Tommy from playing with dolls.

Ethics of Rights, Ethics of Care, and Difference Feminism

And we should also be aware that even attempts to switch these differences around may be harmful; Gilligan (1993) tried to show that women operate under a different kind of ethic than men. Men go about their business using a model of justice and rights; the questions for men are, *Is this fair?* and, *Are my rights being respected?* Women, on the other hand, operate from an ethic of care and mutual responsibility; the question is, *Does this meet the needs of everyone involved?* Gilligan (1993) is attempting to do something important here—she is attempting to describe how men and women experience development differently due to gendered expectations—men have traditionally been expected to manage work and economic productivity, and women have traditionally been expected to manage human relationships and domestic affairs. And it can be argued that this "woman's ethic"—the ethic of mutual care—is in fact better and preferable to an ethic of "every man for himself."

But there is a big problem here. As Pollit (1994) persuasively argued, this kind of "difference feminism," which says that men and women are different and women are in fact better, is ultimately pernicious. Why? Think of the old putting-women-on-a-pedestal idea. Is it fair to expect women to be better than men? Should women be held to a higher standard than men? Clearly, equality should mean the chance to be no better and no worse than anyone else and to have no societal expectations to the contrary. Remember the second shift idea—women are not only expected to work, but they are expected to also keep primary responsibility for the family. Why? Because they are better than men at managing relationships, aren't they? It should be clear why there are documented health benefits to men from marriage (e.g., Lilliard & Panis, 1996) and why many women experience a great deal of stress in balancing their work and personal lives.

And this returns us to the fundamental critique that feminism offers to psychoanalysis (and, indeed, all psychological treatments). The problem, from a feminist point of view, is that Freud looked for complex psychological explanations for many of his female clients, when in many cases simpler explanations from the perspective of gender differences would have done much better—i.e., the subordination of women by culture explains the behavior of women better than Freud's at time torturous interpretations. Shumalith Firestone (1970) saw psychoanalysis as a kind of failure—a failed feminism. In *The Dialectic of Sex,* she said that psychoanalysis and feminism grew out of the same environment, but she said that Freud diagnosed/misdiagnosed something as pathology and offered a doubtful cure, while feminism found the real cause and prescribed the real cure. The real problem wasn't hysterical women, but the lack of opportunity and the way that women at that time were forced to act out in their body the things they could not say or do. She says that far from envying a man his penis, a woman of that time period might envy the power associated with the penis—his ability for social and professional advancement. (This is a brilliant move on her part; if one takes Freud's writings on women and sexuality and substitutes the word "power" whenever he mentions "penis," these passages are magically transformed from the worst things that Freud ever wrote to some of his most perceptive.)

The goal, in the eyes of Firestone (1970), is to stop trying to make women fit into a misogynistic society; individual psychotherapy, in this view, is one more way to do this. Instead, social action is needed, to change this society to accommodate women—and men. And wonderfully enough, this is exactly what happened with Bertha Pappenheim. Recall that Pappenheim suffered through well-meaning but unhelpful attempts of men to change her to fit into her extremely patriarchal family—a family in which the father gave thanks for not being a female. Recall that she was a brilliant person, fluent in many languages, vibrant, intelligent, full of life. And recall that it was only when she was able to focus on making changes on society rather than to focus on making changes on herself that she grew into the amazing person she truly was.

Psychological Adjustment and Societal Change

This is another vital clinical consideration to keep in mind—one more theme that keeps coming back to the field. Psychological adjustment is important, but we must always keep in mind that adjustment to a society that remains racist and misogynistic is problematic. We would do well to once again keep in mind our first patient and what would likely have been much more therapeutic for her: a full, empathic examination of the situation that she was in and how she might work to change it. This does not mean a simplistic opposition between psychological functioning and societal change; in Pappenheim's case, as in the case for us all, there will need to be a balance between healthy individual adjustment to an often-crazy world and active efforts to change what we can. Counseling can serve as a wonderful opportunity to examine just how this can happen in individual lives—to examine the impact of race, culture, gender, and class with every client we see rather than an uncritical reinforcement of supposed differences among human beings.

Summary

- This chapter addressed three major multicultural categories: race/ethnicity, social class, and sex/gender.
- Multiculturalism in counseling is not a mere add-on or an optional feature—Freud's status as a Jew in anti-Semitic Europe provides a visceral reminder that multicultural considerations informed counseling from its inception.
- Freud struggled against racist charges that he had created a degenerate Jewish theory; racism indelibly shaped Freud's experience as a boy growing up and throughout his adult life.
- Ironically, psychoanalysis became identified as a treatment for rich people; it also came to be seen as potentially discriminatory against diverse populations.
- Freud's first concern as a breadwinner was money; however, he also donated time and vouchers that could be used at free clinics of that time.
- Psychoanalysis came to be seen as only something for those with the time (and resources, money and otherwise) to afford it.
- Additionally, it was seen as something needing ego strength—as the thinking went, How could a person who is concerned with making the rent find enough ego energy to fully engage in demanding, insight-oriented treatment?
- Fortunately, relationally oriented theorists have shown that these views are false. Scholars have worked to address race, culture, gender, and class, and there have been extended treatments of the development of psychoanalysis in various parts of the world. Altman provides a wonderful example of how relationally oriented psychoanalysis can be practiced in an urban setting, dispelling the myth of psychoanalysis as a treatment for the rich.
- Feminism provided a critique of psychoanalysis, saying that Freud was misguided—what women of his time needed was not psychological treatment, but economic empowerment!
- Supposed differences between men and women are, in fact, quite small, according to a recent meta-analysis of empirical research.
- Nonetheless, gender differences continue to be talked about; in one view, women can be seen as more nurturing—better—than men, employing an ethic of care and concern for others.
- However, this places a different set of expectations on women (in addition to flying in the face of research that shows small differences between men

and women, and no support for the idea that women operate from an ethic of care).

- As we counsel individuals, we must stay vigilant of gender stereotypes and maintain an awareness that psychological problems take place within a socio-political context that tends to essentialize male and female experience to the detriment of both.

5

A Case Illustration of Contemporary Psychoanalytic Counseling

In order to practically illustrate what actual psychoanalytical clinical practice might look like, let us consider the fictitious case of Jennie Lin. Jennie is a forty-year-old woman of Asian heritage who has two young children, Anabelle, who is five, and Jeremiah, who is nine. She is a successful lawyer and is married to John, age forty-one, who is white and who is a psychotherapist. They live on the outskirts of Baltimore and are financially stable. Jennie's parents live nearby and are very involved in caring for Jennie's children; Jennie's father and mother both came from Taiwan to the United States in young adulthood, and while they have traveled back to their birth country, they tended to downplay the importance of their Asian heritage when Jennie was growing up and did not respond at great length when she asked them questions about Taiwan. Her mother would typically say things like "That's the past" and "You're an American now."

Session One: Getting to Know Jennie

Jennie presents to counseling as depressed. Her husband worried when Jennie stopped arguing with her mother about the raising of their children; when he saw that she gave in to her mother, he insisted that she see a counselor: "He knew something was wrong, big-time, when I just said to

Mom, 'Go ahead, do what you want with them, you will anyway,'" Jennie reports with a wan smile. In response to further questions, Jennie says that she feels a sense of being ashamed a lot in her interpersonal interaction with her husband and her parents and her children. She feels constantly criticized by them. "My husband says it's all in my head. That's pretty great, isn't it—a shrink who says that to his own wife?!" Her father is usually supportive, but in the conflicts between Jennie and her mother, he takes his wife's side—"Of course I get it," Jennie says. "The whole united front."

Her relationship with her mother is also problematic to Jennie. "She's constantly criticizing me. She says I spoil my kids, but then she gives them everything they want. She says I better watch it with John, that if I'm not a better wife—whatever that means—he'll leave me. But then when it's just her and me she'll go on and on about all of John's faults. And I don't know how this has happened, but even my kids criticize me. Anabelle refuses to eat food I make for her, she says that I don't know how to cut her sandwiches right. Jeremiah says that I'm a spaz, and he gets this really pained look on his face whenever I try to talk to his friends. I thought this wasn't supposed to happen until he was a teenager! It seems like everyone takes aim at me," Jennie says.

In addition to exploring her significant relationships—which Jennie appears eager to discuss—her counselor also explores other aspects of her experience. She reports her mood as low, but is able to take pleasure in her children and did recently go out with her husband on a date night, which she reported enjoying. She reported no significant medical issues, aside from painful periods—"my husband jokes that I'm premenstrual for seven days, have my period for seven, and recover from it for another seven, which leaves me seven or eight normal days"—which have been examined but no significant medical issues found. Her sleep is erratic due to Anabelle's wakefulness at night—"guess who's the one who has to get up with her? Me." She reports some fatigue, but finds that she is able to concentrate on work, though she does find herself being forgetful about household things—"I once sent Jeremiah out the door with Anabelle's coat. You can imagine how that went over." She denies suicidal thoughts or plans and reports no history of suicide attempts or ideation. "My mother would kill me if I killed myself," she jokes.

At the end of the first session, she pauses at the door and turns. "You know, it's like I'm wearing a sign that says, Open season—take your best shot!"

Jennie has given her counselor a wonderful first impression of what it is like to be her. And since the relationship between client and counselor is crucial, we must also examine not just who Jennie is, but who the counselor is as well; for the purposes of this example, let us assume that Jennie's counselor is a white male in his middle fifties who practices from a culturally aware, relationally oriented psychoanalytic perspective. From this perspective, her counselor would want to be RESPECTFUL and work on ADDRESSING key cultural issues that D'Andrea and Daniels (2001) and Hays (2008) respectively suggest are essential in delivering diversity competent services. They serve as frameworks for making sure that no key aspects of Jennie's experience are left out—or key aspects of the relationship between Jennie and her counselor.

ADDRESSING JENNIE'S CASE RESPECTFULLY

As we have discussed previously, an important thing to keep in mind always is that certain group memberships will be more salient than others. In other words, for each client, we must not only holistically examine their situation in terms of race/ethnicity, gender, and so on, but also work with our clients to understand how important these memberships are to them and what meanings they derive from them. Here are some aspects of Jennie's case, followed by their salience to Jennie.

Age and Generational Influences, and Gender—as a forty-year-old woman, Jennie occupies a unique age demographic. Born in 1974, she came of age in the 1980s and 1990s in the United States. Huge technological shifts occurred, including the rise of video games, personal computers and the Internet, momentous political shifts, including the fall of the Berlin Wall and the dissolution of the Soviet Union, and social and cultural developments.

- Jennie strongly identifies with her "forty-something" female peers. She is highly aware that she falls in a female demographic that achieved highly in career terms, building on the career successes of women who went before her. At least, the success of some women. Her own mother didn't work outside the home, and this fact appears to cause a great deal of mutual misunderstanding.

Religious and Spiritual Beliefs—Jennie's parents identify with religious beliefs and practices that comprise four dominant traditions: Buddhism, Confucianism, and Daoism, and traditional Chinese religious practices (Poceski, 2009), and they hold beliefs that stress harmonious, hierarchical relations among family members (Sue & Sue, 2008) and holistic balance of the life energy, Qi, to achieve spiritual, social, and physical health (Park, 2011).

- Jennie herself is unclear what her own beliefs are; she tends to talk about her beliefs in the context of what her parents believe and what her husband believes. She didn't fully identify with her parents' beliefs, but doesn't fully identify with her husband's Protestant Christian beliefs either. While she did not initially list religious issues as important to address, she has spoken increasingly of the link between her depression and a feeling of a spiritual void in her life.

Race/Ethnicity and National Origin—Jennie's parents emigrated from Taiwan before she was born; they spoke Mandarin and identify as Han. Since coming to the United States, however, her parents consistently play down their past.

(Continued)

(Continued)

- Once again, Jennie is left uncertain about what her exact status is, in this case vis-à-vis her ethnic heritage. Not only that, she is unclear how important this is or should be to her. The multiculturally aware counselor would want to be familiar with racial/cultural identity models, in particular those relating to Asian American identity (Sue & Sue, 2008). In fact, this sense of a yet-to-be-developed identity may be a key theme that could help Jennie understand her situation and may be a way for her to integrate her various disparate issues with her children, her husband, and her parents. What is her identity? What models are available to her that might help her further develop her wonderfully unique identity? Are there resources she could identify—books, movies, friends and acquaintances, Internet sources—that might help her? How might a family trip to Taiwan help Jennie and her family understand themselves?

Jennie's multiple roles—as a working woman, a daughter of Asian immigrants, a wife, and a mother—appear to be interacting with her presenting problem of depression. Her counselor, aware of the persistence of the second shift phenomenon (Hochschild & Machung, 2012), asks her questions about how she balances love—her relationships with her parents, husband, and children—with work—her fulfilling identity as a successful lawyer. In listening to her responses, he adopts the position that Freud suggested, listening not only for clues about her cognitive strategies and preferred mechanisms of defense, but also listening with his unconscious empathically attuned to her. From his relational perspective, he listens, in effect, to the music underlying the words that she speaks, because it is this music that will convey the unconscious tone and timbre of her experience.

Sessions Two to Four: The Growth of the Counseling Relationship

From the beginning of session two to the end of session four, the counselor feels that their counseling relationship has begun to assume some importance to Jennie. In session two, she reports that she discussed parts of their first session with her husband: "He says you made a nice reframe when you said that I'm stepping back so that others can step forward." And, halfway through the third session, Jennie pauses and remarks, "That's a nice shirt, by the way. My dad has one just like it." As might be expected, her counselor finds these comments interesting. Is her husband regarding Jennie's new counselor as a rival? Is she suggesting that she is beginning to see her counselor in the role of a father to her?

No matter one's theoretical orientation, a third session is not a twenty-third session. Because it is so early in treatment, her counselor does not remark on her comments. *Takt,* which Freud prized, comprises an awareness of the subtle timing inherent in the therapeutic enterprise, in which saying something too soon is a risk to be avoided. Rather, her counselor notes them and retunes his unconscious receptively toward her; to continue the radio metaphor, he may have received signals on a particular wavelength, and he continues to scan to see if this is a station that he can pick up again.

Sessions Five and Six: The Usual Detours

In counseling, things rarely progress in a straightforward fashion, and Jennie comes in for session five eager to talk about something entirely different. It is very common for counseling to take repeated detours, and the counselor listens closely to the concerns that Jennie has with Anabelle—Anabelle has developed facial tics, and Jennie wonders what to do about it. They discuss the situation in detail for two sessions and discover a few interesting facts. The tics are much worse when it's just Jennie and Anabelle; John, her husband, is unconcerned with them; and Jennie's grandmother thinks that it is due to an imbalance of Qi and wants Annabelle to visit an acupuncturist. (When Annabelle heard this, she yelled, "They should stick needles in Grandma instead of me!" which didn't endear her to her grandmother, who said that it was further evidence how spoiled Jennie's children were.) After exploring a number of options, Jennie and her counselor agree that the best thing for her to do is to ignore the tics; sometimes commonsense ideas such as "it's just a phase that she'll grow out of" are often the best to follow.

Session Seven: The Big Dream

In the seventh session, Jennie reports having a dream. She says that she's wearing one of her daughter's dresses. Her family—her parents, her husband, and her children—are around but seem to be ignoring her. She tries to get them to notice her. "It's kind of like I'm three years old, throwing a tantrum, and then when everyone turns and look at me, I wake up."

This dream seems highly significant, and from a Freudian perspective, this dream holds much promise in helping articulate what is going on outside of Jennie's conscious awareness—not only the content of the dream, but also the fact that she is so eager to talk about it. The counselor uses empathic listening to fully explore the dream. As he does so, he becomes aware of the undercurrents and unspoken context of the dream. In the dream, she is the child; everyone else is the grownup, including her children. In the dream, she wants attention but can't get it in an adult fashion, but must revert to childish expression. She wants attention, but when she gets it—when all the faces of her family turns to her, it is unbearable to her and she wakes up—"My heart is pounding and my mind is blank," Jennie says.

Having had a number of sessions with Jennie, the counselor begins to form a set of possible interpretations. From a contemporary position that is informed by Schore's (1994) implicit affective self model, the counselor hypothesizes that Jennie's dream isn't just telling her that she feels like a three-year-old, but something more specific. She might be experiencing difficulty in managing the intense flooding of emotion that takes place when one both desires human contact and attention—and when one actually *gets* this contact and attention.

It is a common experience for humans to fantasize about being famous and adored by multitudes; it is also common for many of us to turn beet red when a group of people turn and stare at us. Thus Jennie's problem is both a concrete problem of how to regulate one's response in both the absence and the presence of human contact, as well as a larger, existential issue in which she is perhaps struggling with the idea of whether it is even possible to fruitfully engage other people—a deep struggle that may be tied to her depression. After all, it is one thing to desire human contact, it is another to be uncomfortable with it when it happens, but it is an entirely different thing to wonder whether human contact—getting it or not getting it—is worth the stress and strain that it engenders.

Moreover, with a perspective that is informed by Sue and Sue's (2008) description of the collectivist, hierarchically oriented, more directive and authoritarian parenting styles, and discouragement of strong emotionality of traditional Asian cultures and Asian Americans who have these cultural values, the counselor might also hypothesize that Jennie is experiencing a common, stressful conflict between European values and non-European values that has played out in a complex fashion in her family of origin and continuing into her marriage with John. There may have been instances in Jennie's past where she wanted attention and was discouraged by her parents from expressing this need in this particular way; had Jennie grown up in Taiwan, she would have been surrounded by circumstances that would've helped her understand her parents' response.

In the United States, however, the contemporary parenting response tends to be one of accommodation to a child's expressions of need—perhaps even to an overaccommodation. In Taiwan, in the context of other families who responded like her parents did, Jennie would've had overt and covert information to help her process her experience—*Oh, I see, this is how my friends' parents respond to their children when they do things like I do. It makes sense that my parents responded to me like this, that's just how parents respond to children.* With this information, she would've had the normalizing experience of being like all her friends. Instead, in the United States, she may have been confused, if her peers' families seemed to encourage rather than seem to discourage individual expressions of emotional needs—*This is weird, when my friends start to cry and throw fits, their parents rush over and are all over them, but when I do it, it's like my parents' faces turn to stone.* Thus her cultural background may interact with her developmental experience of attempting to understand and modulate her emotional responses.

Her counselor also thinks about Jennie's relationship with her mother. Clearly, Jennie and her mother deeply value and love each other. However, the intersection of Jennie's career with her children, husband, and her parents, especially her mother, is very complex. In one sense, it subverts the traditional views of the hierarchy in a family, with the man (and his work) taking precedence; in Jennie's case, her job is as important as her husband's (and financially, it is in fact quite a bit more so). Jennie's mother has a hard time understanding the negotiation that goes on between Jennie and her husband; in Jennie's mother's view, the solution should invariably be that Jennie compromise (i.e., give up her position). When this doesn't occur, Jennie's mother feels uneasy and wonders about Jennie's adoption of masculine rights and prerogatives (and she also wonders about Jennie's husband's adoption of what seems to her as a feminine role). Jennie alternates between feeling defiant of her mother and guilt-ridden, which tends to worsen her feelings of depression.

All these things are in his mind as he talks with her about her dream. She tells him that when she woke up, she found Anabelle snuggled up to her—as soon as Jennie opened her eyes, Anabelle said, "Pancakes—on the double!"

"I know I shouldn't encourage her, but it's hard not to laugh," Jennie says ruefully. "I told Anabelle that it was daddy's turn, but she just said, 'The big guy isn't getting up any time soon and you know it.'"

At this the counselor laughs, and they share a few stories about the funny (and inappropriate) things that children can say.

"Once," the counselor says, "as I was carrying my daughter out of the store—she was having a major meltdown—she yelled, *Somebody call social services!* Talk about strange looks. I was saying to everybody, *I'm a counselor, really, I'm a counselor*. She was five."

Those who identify with the tradition that emphasizes Freud's statements on abstinence and neutrality would be shocked by this self-disclosure; more relationally oriented psychoanalysts would say that such self-disclosure can inestimably strengthen the therapeutic relationship. And indeed Jennie appears relieved that the counselor—a professional like herself—would have the same problems as she had. Significantly, she starts to complain that Annabelle is right and that John rarely gets up in the morning.

This is a significant piece of information for her counselor. From a feminist perspective, her counselor is approaching counseling itself warily. Is Jennie's "depression problem" really the problem? Is it perhaps the case that the problem isn't Jennie's, but the inequitable arrangement that she's been forced to accept? As frequently happens, even with well-educated couples such as Jennie and John, housework and childrearing still falls disproportionately on the female, even when both work equally outside the home. In Jennie's case, it does appear that the second shift is alive and well. As a result of working more and harder, she may be getting rundown, not sleeping enough, and not taking care of herself—all of which may be significantly impacting her mood.

After she lists a few more complaints—that John thinks that organizing the garage counts as housework and that he tends to be suspiciously sloppy with washing clothes, which leads Jennie to just do it all herself—the counselor asks, with a carefully neutral tone, "Could you tell me a little more about how you and your husband structure housework and the care of your children?"

Immediately, Jennie defends her husband: "John really helps me out with the kids," she says. "Really, he is a big help."

The counselor notes that Jennie uses the defensive strategy of denial when she tries to show that their relationship equally divides these tasks; to the counselor, Jennie is clearly doing much more than John. And as a feminist, her counselor notes this language—her husband is "helping" her. This assumes that she has the primary role, and John's role is as a support to her. Has this ever been discussed by the two of them? Is this a fair distribution? Jennie may be denying this inequality and unfairness, but her counselor recognizes that this denial is serving a vital function—it protects her from the painful idea that her husband, who loves her, is allowing her to become rundown and even ill from taking on more than her fair share. Rather than try to force her to this insight, the counselor is quite careful, because unknown consequences may arise if Jennie truly sees the fact.

Knowing this, he is careful to let go of this line of inquiry—for the time being. Before denial can be replaced with something more ultimately functional, the counselor needs to collaboratively accomplish the task Freud set out so many years ago—to help strengthen Jennie's Ego to functionally and directly address the daunting tasks ahead of it. Jennie has to find a way to address her mother, who comes from a cultural perspective in which fulfilling one's obligations to one's parents is of crucial importance. She needs to have the hard conversations with her husband about equality and justice.

She needs to find the strength to stand up to her kids, which can be a challenge to any parent. These are incredibly hard things to do.

Her mother loves Jennie but has her own rich developmental and cultural history, one that may find it hard to accept feedback from Jennie about her mother's involvement with her grandchildren. Her husband, no matter how nice a man he is, isn't likely to thank her for asking him to work harder in their relationship and with their children. Her children have already developed some patterned (mis)behavior with her, and changing this will require careful and consistent reinforcement on her part—never easy for a parent, especially one like Jennie who also has outside work obligations and comes home exhausted and may not have the energy to fight important battles with them.

At the end of the session, the counselor feels tired; by the way she walks to the door, he guesses that Jennie feels the same. Yet when she turns and faces him to thank him, he is interested to find not just tiredness in her eyes, but some relief, as if it was indeed a help to let these things out.

Session Eight: How Should I Respond?

In between the seventh and eighth sessions, the counselor muses about how to respond to Jennie. The big dream sparked a discussion and a lot of thoughts and responses in the counselor; the big dream evokes a big imaginative response. He remembers that Jennie reacted with some defensiveness when he gently asked her about her relationship with John and with her mother. He asks himself, *How should I respond to her?* Rather than trying to work it out beforehand, he simply asks this question and lets his unconscious work on it during the week.

When they meet for session eight, Jennie brings in another, unrelated issue, this time about Jeremiah. "He just seems pretty listless, not himself. Crying for no reason. Very clingy."

"You appear concerned about his behavior."

"I am. A little. I wonder if he's depressed."

"What does your husband think of this?"

"The usual. He says I'm overreacting. Says it's just part of normal childhood development."

The counselor interprets this as a wish on Jennie's part to help him understand her struggle. He senses that this is an instance in which she might be wishing for contact with him. There seems to be a special longing look in her eyes, and his gut tells him that she wants something from him, though he doesn't know exactly what it is. She seems near tears, and her emotion, so quick in the session—only a couple of minutes have passed—is not so much inappropriate as much differently expressed from prior sessions. He asks himself, *What does my evenly suspended attention* (which is what Freud said should be the attitude of the clinician) *tell me about her attention and interest in me and our relationship, right here and right now?*

Before he makes any more comments, the moment is over, and Jennie recovers with a laugh. She talks the rest of the session—a little more rapidly, a little more animatedly than she has in other sessions. She decides that her husband is right—she is overreacting—and, significantly, she thanks the counselor for helping her come to this conclusion (in reality, he did nothing to help her move toward this conclusion). As she stands up to leave, her look is quite different from last time—a little hooded, a little protected.

Session Nine: The Time Is Right

A few minutes into the next session, Jennie's counselor gets the unmistakable feeling that the time is right to bring up some of the thoughts that he has been having. It might be the fact that she does not bring anything new up; it might also be the fact that she appears to be looking to him to initiate the conversation. It might be that when she looks at him, she appears somewhat expectant, open, if a little unsure. He simply gets the impression that she wishes to hear from him.

"You know," he begins, "when you left the session last week, it seemed like you were looking at me like, *I wonder if he gets it? I wonder if he will be just like my husband and think I'm always overreacting.*"

Jennie pauses before she replies. "I don't know if I was exactly thinking that. I mean, not then. I did think it earlier."

"What were you thinking then?"

"You'll think I'm crazy," Jennie bursts out.

Wordlessly, they look each other—then both laugh.

"Is that what you were thinking then—or now?" her counselor asks.

"Now. Well and maybe then, too. When I looked at you, I was just thinking, *Does he really listen to his wife? Really listen?* I'm sorry, I don't mean to be a jerk."

It is an amazing moment. Her counselor gets the sense that she is serious, she really is curious—and at the same time, she appears fearful that she has offended him—fearful to be in contact with him in such an intimate way.

"You are concerned that I might think that you are jerk for wondering that?"

"Well, yes."

"Could you tell me a little more about your concern?"

An artless question—but it isn't so much what was said as the fact that both affectively and cognitively, Jennie and her counselor are attuned to one another. Jennie opens up. She senses that he is truly interested in her thoughts and emotions and in helping her look at her life and the unhelpful patterns that she seems to get herself into. She senses that he is not particularly interested in changing any of these patterns—rather, he is primarily interested in knowing whether he is understanding her in a way that is helpful to her.

In the conversation that follows, her counselor also openly describes his own failures in listening to his wife; as with the other time that he self-disclosed about his daughter, Jennie appears greatly relieved. She describes how she would like to be able to talk to John more openly, but she says that he always appears too tired to talk. "I mean, he listens to people's problems all day, just like you do, and I don't blame him if he doesn't want to hear my complaining when he gets home."

Increasingly, her counselor is able to give her feedback in real time about how he is understanding her struggle. He shares his impression of her dream—that it may be giving her important information about her desire for human care and attention, and her ambivalent attitude toward receiving it. He provides the normalizing perspective that many people experience highly ambivalent attitudes as well and says that we seem to both intensely need human contact but can find it hard to fully enjoy it when we get it. He also suggests that there may be a cultural component and shares his hypothesis of how she may have been a little confused by the difference in her mom and dad's parenting style with that of her peers' families. He wonders if she might sometimes experience her interactions with her family—with her mother, with her husband, with her children—not from the perspective as a grown, competent, mature woman, but as an ashamed young child.

At this last statement, Jennie visibly sat up. "That's exactly it."

"How does that make you feel?"

She turns her gaze upon her counselor—there is look of determination in her eyes. "Like I don't want to be an ashamed little girl anymore."

Session Ten (and Beyond): On the Journey, Together

From a common factors perspective, her counselor is focused on Jennie and their relationship; he knows that the theory he is bringing to their work together is useful only inasmuch as it makes sense to Jennie and helps her. Over the course of their next sessions, they pursue the idea that Jennie is working toward fully experiencing herself as a competent adult. When it is appropriate, her counselor wonders—would it be helpful to address instances in counseling where Jennie might feel that her counselor is critical of Jennie's behavior—and so risk repeating how she is being treated in her outside relationships? Would it be helpful to talk about a pattern that he seems to observe, in which she acts in ways to become close to people (such as asking him if he really listens to his wife) but then immediately experiences shame and apologizes (which is how he interprets her statement about being a jerk for asking)? Would it be helpful to explore her thoughts and behavior that seem self-defeating, such as failing to achieve a sense of herself in her family as a confident, strong woman—the person she is at her workplace, where she is a highly successful and respected member of her group practice?

In doing so, the counselor is less concerned with being right or correct with his interpretations—he is much more concerned with how his comments appear to strike Jennie's receptive unconscious. Were there changes in her posture or gaze when he said certain things—like when she reacted to his statement about her being an ashamed little girl? Is she receptive to still further comments—and can he be open as well, modeling how one might receive comments about oneself in real time? He is especially careful to avoid the interpretive excesses that Freud was sometimes prone to, including a dogmatic insistence on sexuality as the root cause of neurotic behavior. Rather, he focuses on coconstructing interpretations of her behavior that make sense to her and that appear to hold promise for adaptive change. There is a strong pragmatism in his approach, in which the ultimate value is whether an interpretation appears to work and be useful in their work together.

Summary

- From a relational perspective, the process of treatment with Jennie will comprise aspects of a reparenting relationship at a deeply unconscious level.
- In their work, the counselor must be aware of the possibility of harm, as has been repeatedly emphasized and which was foreseen by Freud when he discussed the possibility of remolding our clients in our own image.
- Instead of attempting to remake clients in our image, the model is of optimal parenting, in which the true concern is to help the child grow and develop into their own person, not carbon copies of the parent.
- In doing so, he will help her toward insights that are dynamic and that can be acted on rationally.
- Though it may be a cliché, the destination is not as important as their journey together—what is important for Jennie is to face her life not with all the answers, but with more satisfying and varied interpersonal strategies, with a stronger sense that she is in charge and capable to address her very complex life—to know that what she thought of as unattainable and impossible is child's play for her mature ego now.

6
Conclusion

In this book, we have seen how the contemporary psychoanalytic practitioner operates from a common factors perspective, putting client and relationship first. She does this knowing the important, relational updating of the approach that examines the interaction of counselor and client within a sociocultural context. She knows that to use Freud, we must be open to updating him; to use the metaphor that a counseling theory is like a roadmap, telling us how we might travel with the client from Point A to Point B, we must periodically update the roadmap, accounting for new roads, new interchanges, new restaurants to sample and new hotels to stay at. There's no reason to use an outdated map if a new one will help us travel more effectively through the landscape.

The Unconscious, Version 2.0

For example, in looking at the idea of the unconscious, we find that it can indeed give us insight into the behavior of people in our personal lives as well as public figures. One of the guilty pleasures in presenting the unconscious to counselors-in-training is the certainty that our public figures will provide a never-ending stream of examples of less-than-rational behavior. The unconscious appears alive and well when crime-fighting public crusaders against prostitution are charged with using escort services. But again, we don't need to treat Freud's views on the unconscious or any other concept as beyond dispute. Freud considered himself a scientist, and he would approve of the continual scientific examination of claims and hypotheses about our mental life. The question of the empirical status of the unconscious, not surprisingly, continues to be discussed and debated, but there does appear substantial support for its existence. Westen (1999) asserts that "a large body of experimental research has emerged in a number of independent literatures. This work documents the most fundamental tenet of psychoanalysis—that much of mental life is unconscious, including cognitive, affective, and motivational processes" (p. 1061). Bargh and Morsella (2006) state that "contemporary social cognition research... [demonstrates] the existence of sophisticated, flexible, and adaptive unconscious behavior guidance systems" (p. 78). Cramer (2000) asserts that "virtually every leading cognitive psychologist today accepts the premise that mental processes go on outside of awareness" (p. 638).

But crucial changes need to be made to Freud's views, including changes that alter them significantly. As Schore (2003) says, "instead of a repository of archaic untamed passions and destructive wishes, the unconscious is now seen as a cohesive, active mental structure that continuously appraises life's experiences and responds according to its scheme of interpretation. And in contrast to a static, deeply buried storehouse of ancient memories buried and silenced in 'infantile amnesia,' contemporary intersubjective psychoanalysts now refer to a 'relational unconscious,' whereby one unconscious mind communicates with another unconscious mind" (p. xvi). Thus we now understand the unconscious to be much more creative and helpful (points made by Jung [1961] and throughout Milton Erickson's work on hypnosis and trance induction [Haley, 1986]), a dynamic force that the contemporary counselor's own unconscious can ally with to produce positive therapeutic change.

Furthermore, the concept of the unconscious must be updated in light of multicultural critiques such as Brickman (2003) who demonstrate that Freud's view of the "primitive" unconscious partook of Western European ethnocentric biases. In this view, Freud did indeed subvert traditional Western views of cultural superiority when he said that "both civilized and primitive shared an underlying psychism, which civilized humans would never transcend once and for all" (Brickman, 2003, p. 88). However, Freud also reproduced Western biases by equating the unconscious, which is characterized by "a lack of rationality, a lack of relationship to reality, an inability to represent itself in words, a lack of restraint, sexual and otherwise, a lack of morality, and a lack of the sense of time" (p. 81) with so-called primitive societies and primitive man. This persistently ethnocentric (i.e., thinking that the West is a more evolved culture than non-Western cultures) and dubiously evolutionary (i.e., thinking of modern cultures as inherently more advanced that cultures in the past) biases must be addressed, lest the contemporary counselor uncritically reproduce these errors by speaking glibly about the unconscious as a "regressive, infantile, and pathological place" (Mattei, 2008, p. 248) that can be compared to noncontemporary, non-Western cultures.

A More Useful Freud

Thus we might find ourselves agreeing with Freud that unconscious life is important, but disagreeing with him on how exactly to characterize that life. Reinterpretation is vital, which often takes the form of softening Freud's view. This has been the de facto strategy employed by those who have followed after him. Erikson (1963), for example, famously said that Freud's dictum for a fulfilled life was "'lieben und arbeiten' (to love and to work)" (p. 265). However, as has been pointed out, Freud never said this (Elms, 2001). It was in fact part of Erikson's project to make Freud more accessible (more user-friendly, in today's terms) and developmentally appropriate (e.g., his rendering of Freud's psychosexual stages into the Eight Ages of Man). In doing this, Erikson helps us understand Jennie Lin's experience as a woman who is trying to juggle multiple complex roles, addressing the key crucial young middle-age task of balancing care and love for her parents and husband and children with work obligations.

The project of making use of Freud's contributions while simultaneously modifying them into more useful forms is ongoing. One of the assertions I make to my students is that contemporary counselors, along with the general public, hold a softened or modified view of many of Freud's concepts. The unconscious is a prime example. Most counselors, along with their clients, believe that people "have" an unconscious, and that certain behaviors are motivated by it, but few hold that it motivates all behavior, and few believe it motivates no behavior. The unconscious, softened, modified, yet still potent, serves as an important topic of inquiry for counselors-in-training. An inquiry into the unconscious asks, *To what degree do you believe people are motivated by unconscious thoughts and wishes?* and, *To what degree, and in what ways, can counselors help people gain control over these desires?* Clients, and people in general, often act in ways that are inexplicable, and Freud's theories of motivation and control provide a good starting point for counselors-in-training and for counseling itself to begin to explain the seemingly inexplicable.

The Client Is the Most Important Person in the Room

While updating and revising, we must continually return to the fundamental truth that our clients are the most vital common factor and that it is their capacities for self-healing and growth that drives counseling

(Bohart, 2000). We must continually remind ourselves that the counseling relationship is the vehicle for change, transporting client and counselor along their mutually agreed-upon path to their mutually agreed-upon destination. The relationship doesn't just contain the interventions that the theory suggests; it is also the single most important intervention itself. In the case of Jennie, she will likely remember the general tone of the work she did with her counselor long after she has forgotten most of the specifics. She will remember a compassionate look in her counselor's eye, a time when he looked at her instead of away from her, a time when he held her gaze and it felt to her like he was physically holding her and supporting her even as she felt like she might fall apart.

If she does remember specific things that her counselor said and did, she will likely remember words and actions that conveyed trust, affection, care, and (dare we say it?) love. Professional love, love that will never be sexual and that will never be exploitative or self-serving. Perhaps the love that Martin Luther King (1957/1986) referred to as *agape* love, *agape* being a Greek word for a kind of selfless love that could create a nonviolent beloved community that Dr. King strove for and gave his life for. If it is true that the counseling relationship heals in part through its reactivation of the parenting relationship, then if it is to be therapeutic this relationship must be characterized by a fundamental care and full acceptance of the client that may or may not have been present in the original parenting setting. We ask our clients to do something amazing—we ask them to change in front of our eyes. In return, it doesn't seem to be too much to ask that we should strive for the kind of love that effective parents have when they watch their children try, in Nietzsche's (1887/1974) words, to become who they are.

Future Considerations

We must also continue to practice self- and other awareness and to embrace and celebrate the full diversity of humanity. We must be self-aware and self-analytical (something that Freud preached and tried to practice himself), while always acknowledging Freud's fundamental insight that we are continually deluding ourselves and failing to be fully aware of our innermost motivations. We need to acknowledge that our lack of awareness as a profession has produced, and continues to produce, actual damage to our clients. It is likely that, just as we look back a hundred years and gasp at the barbarity of their attitudes toward the mentally ill, so in a hundred years they will be shaking their heads at our woefully inadequate and downright harmful attitudes and interventions.

As Freud suggested, our rationality is a hope, albeit a slight one, that we can come to a greater awareness of our personal and professional motivations; the less aware we are of these motivations, the greater the potential damage to our clients.

From a psychoanalytic perspective, we must be accepting, tolerant, and attuned to diversity, since our Earth is filled with billions of people who want the same things that we want, who have the same desires and wishes, who are trying to balance the unrealistic desires of their internal Id with the often cruel realities of the external world. Indeed from a Freudian point of view, we are not abiding by the fundamental rules of a democratic society—that there should be no favorites. There are clear favorites regarding wealth and privilege, and this is fundamentally unfair. Reason and rationality should guide us, and it is nowhere clear that allowing great disparities in wealth and privilege is wise from a rational, self-interested perspective, let alone from an ethical perspective.

Thus, while we are working individually with our clients, we must never lose sight of the cultural settings in which our clients and we ourselves nest. In working with clients, diversity competent psychoanalytic practice will be aware of the history of counseling and therapy and its first client, Bertha Pappenheim, who had to struggle out from under societal restraints in order to thrive. Her case asks us to recognize that our well-meaning efforts may have negative consequences and to realize that in our quest to do good, we may in fact do harm. It also asks us to be realistic in our assessment of the basic difficulty of living and the kind of cure we can offer to our clients, while being open to the amazing resilience of former clients who go on to do great things in the world.

Summary

- If we choose to practice from a psychoanalytic perspective, we need to do so from a contemporary place, knowing that Freud's individual drive theory has been revised by attachment theory, object relations, and relational psychoanalysis, developments that have powerfully redefined how people fall ill from a psychoanalytic perspective and how to help them heal in counseling.
- It has also been revised in light of contemporary neuroscience, which furnishes further evidence of the way brain and behavior develop in the context of social relationships.
- These revisions suggest that people fall ill in the context of unhelpful or inadequate primary relationships, and the cure is found by helping people experience exactly what they did not have—a compassionate, observing presence who can help the client identify dysfunctional ways of relating to others that have grown out of past experiences and to provide a kind of wise reparenting in the context of counseling.

- In doing this, these revisions make the point that has been repeatedly emphasized in *Psychoanalytic Approaches for Counselors*—that healing takes place within the therapeutic relationship inaugurated by Freud so many years ago and that just as people can be damaged in the context of relationships with others, so they can be helped to heal in the context of a particular kind of relationship, the counseling relationship.

References

Ahn, H., & Wampold, B. E. (2001). Where oh where are the specific ingredients? A meta-analysis of component studies in counseling and psychotherapy. *Journal of Counseling Psychology, 48,* 251–257. doi: 10.1037//0022-OI67.48.3.251

Altman, N. (2010). *The analyst in the inner city: Race, class and culture through a psychoanalytic lens* (2nd ed.). New York, NY: Routledge.

American Psychiatric Association. (1973). *Homosexuality and sexual orientation disturbance: Proposed change in DSM-II* (6th ed., p. 44). Retrieved from http://www.psychiatryonline.com/DSMPDF/DSM-II_Homosexuality_Revision.pdf

Anderson, H., & Goolishian, H. (1992). The client is the expert: A not-knowing approach to therapy. In S. McNamee & K. J. Gergen (Eds.), *Social construction and the therapeutic process* (pp. 117–136). London, England: Sage.

Appignanesi, L., & Forrester, J. (1992). *Freud's women.* New York, NY: Basic Books.

Bargh, J. A., & Morsella, E. (2008). The unconscious mind. *Perspectives on Psychological Science, 3, 73–79.*

Bayer, R. (1981). *Homosexuality and American psychiatry: The politics of diagnosis.* New York, NY: Basic Books.

Bettleheim, B. (1982). *Freud and man's soul: An important reinterpretation of Freudian theory.* New York, NY: Vintage.

Bohart, A. C. (2000). The client is the most important common factor: Client's self-healing capacities and psychotherapy. *Journal of Psychotherapy Integration, 10,* 127–149. doi: 10.1023/A:100944413210

Breger, L. (2001). *Freud: Darkness in the midst of vision.* New York, NY: Wiley.

Breuer, J., & Freud, S. (1955). Studies on hysteria. In J. Strachey (Ed. & Trans.), *The standard edition of the complete psychological works of Sigmund Freud* (Vol. 2, pp. 1–307). London, England: Hogarth Press. (Original work published 1893–1895)

Brickman, C. (2003). *Aboriginal populations in the mind: Race and primitivity in psychoanalysis.* New York, NY: Columbia University Press.

Browning, C. R. (1992). *Ordinary men: Reserve Police Battalion 101 and the final solution in Poland.* New York, NY: HarperCollins.

Clark, A. J. (1998). *Defense mechanisms in the counseling process.* Thousand Oaks, CA: Sage.

Conyers, L. M. (2002). Disability: An emerging topic in multicultural counseling. In J. Trusty, E. J. Looby, & D. S. Sandhu, (Eds.), *Multicultural counseling: Context, theory and practice, and competence* (pp. 173–202). Huntington, NY: Nova Science Publishers.

Cramer, P. (2000). Defense mechanisms in psychology today: Further processes in adaptation. *American Psychologist, 55,* 637–646. doi: 10.1037//0003-066X.55.6.637

Crews, F. (1986). *Skeptical engagements.* Oxford, England: Oxford University.

Crews, F. (1995). *The memory wars: Freud's legacy in dispute.* New York, NY: New York Review of Books.

D'Andrea, M., & Daniels, J. (2001). RESPECTFUL counseling: An integrative multidimensional model for counselors. In D. B. Pope-Davis & H. L. K. Coleman (Eds.), *The intersection of race, class, and gender in multicultural counseling* (pp. 417–466). Thousand Oaks, CA: Sage.

Damasio, A. R. (1994). *Descartes error: Emotion, reason, and the human brain.* New York, NY: Putnam.

Danto, E. A. (2005). *Freud's free clinics: Psychoanalysis & social justice, 1918–1938.* New York, NY: Columbia University.

Davidson, R. J. (2000). Cognitive neuroscience needs affective neuroscience (and vice versa). *Brain and Cognition, 42,* 89–92. doi: 10.1006/brcg.1999.1170

De Paula Ramos, S. (2003). Revisiting Anna O.: A case of chemical dependence. *History of Psychology, 6,* 239–250. doi: 10.1037/1093–4510.6.3.239

Doolittle, H. (1956). *Tribute to Freud.* New York, NY: Stratford.

Douglas, E. M., & Finkelhor, D. (2005). *Childhood sexual abuse fact sheet: Crimes against children.* Durham: Research Center University of New Hampshire.

Duncan, B. L. (2002). The legacy of Saul Rosenzweig: The profundity of the Dodo bird. *Journal of Psychotherapy Integration, 12,* 32–57. doi: 10.1037//1053-0479.12.1.32

Duncan, B. L., & Miller, S. (2000). *The heroic client.* San Francisco, CA: Jossey-Bass.

Ellenberger, H. E. (1970). *The discovery of the unconscious: The history and evolution of dynamic psychiatry.* New York, NY: Basic Books.

Elms, A. C. (2001). Apocryphal Freud: Sigmund Freud's most famous "quotations" and their actual sources. *Annual of Psychoanalysis, 29,* 83–104.

Erdelyi, M. H. (2006). The unified theory of repression. *Behavioral and Brain Sciences, 29,* 499–551. Retrieved from http://www.wjh.harvard.edu/~wegner/pdfs/Erdelyi%20(2006)%20in%20BBS.pdf

Erikson, E. (1963). *Childhood and society* (2nd ed.). New York, NY: Norton.

Finkelhor, D. (1994). Current information on the scope and nature of child sexual abuse. *The Future of Children, 4,* 31–53.

Finkelhor, D., & Jones, L. M. (2004). *Explanations for the decline in child sexual abuse cases.* Washington, DC: U.S. Department of Justice, Office of Justice Programs, Office of Juvenile Justice and Delinquency Prevention.

Firestone, S. (1970). *The dialectic of sex: The case for feminist revolution.* New York, NY: Farrar, Straus, & Giroux.

Freud, A. (1993). *The Ego and the mechanisms of defence.* London, England: Karnac. (Original work published 1936)

Freud, E. (Ed.). (1992). *The letters of Sigmund Freud* (T. & J. Stern, Trans.). New York, NY: Dover. (Original work published 1960)

Freud, S. (1953). Three essays on the theory of sexuality. In J. Strachey (Ed. & Trans.), *The standard edition of the complete psychological works of Sigmund Freud* (Vol. 7, pp. 130–243). London: Hogarth Press. (Original work published 1905)

Freud, S. (1953a). The interpretation of dreams. In J. Stachey (Ed. & Trans.), *The standard edition of the complete psychological works of Sigmund Freud* (Vol. IV, pp. ix–338). London, England: Hogarth Press. (Original work published 1900)

Freud, S. (1953b). The interpretation of dreams. In J. Stachey (Ed. & Trans.), *The standard edition of the complete psychological works of Sigmund Freud* (Vol. V, pp. 339–627). London, England: Hogarth Press. (Original work published 1900)

Freud, S. (1955). Lines in advance in psycho-analytic therapy. In J. Strachey (Ed. & Trans.), *The standard edition of the complete psychological works of Sigmund Freud* (Vol. 17, pp. 157–168). London: Hogarth Press. (Original work published 1919)

Freud, S. (1955). Two encyclopaedia articles: A psycho-analysis. In J. Strachey (Ed. & Trans.), *The standard edition of the complete psychological works of Sigmund Freud* (Vol. 18, pp. 235–254). London: Hogarth Press. (Original work published 1923)

Freud, S. (1957). On the history of the psychoanalytic movement. In J. Stachey (Ed. & Trans.), *The standard edition of the complete psychological works of Sigmund Freud* (Vol. 14, pp. 7–66). London, England: Hogarth Press. (Original work published 1914)

Freud, S. (1958). A note on the unconscious in psycho-analysis. In J. Stachey (Ed. & Trans.), *The standard edition of the complete psychological works of Sigmund Freud* (Vol. 12, pp. 260–266). London: Hogarth Press. (Original work published 1912)

Freud, S. (1958). Observations on transference-love. In J. Stachey (Ed. & Trans.), *The standard edition of the complete psychological works of Sigmund Freud* (Vol. 12, pp. 157–173). London: Hogarth Press. (Original work published 1915)

Freud, S. (1959). An autobiographical study. In J. Stachey (Ed. & Trans.), *The standard edition of the complete psychological works of Sigmund Freud* (Vol. 20, pp. 7–70). London, England: Hogarth Press. (Original work published 1925)

Freud, S. (1960). Jokes and their relation to the unconscious. In J. Stachey (Ed. & Trans.), *The standard edition of the complete psychological works of Sigmund Freud* (Vol. 8, pp. 3–258). London, England: Hogarth Press. (Original work published 1905)

Freud, S. (1960). The psychopathology of everyday life. In J. Stachey (Ed. & Trans.), *The standard edition of the complete psychological works of Sigmund Freud* (Vol. 6, pp. 1–310). London, England: Hogarth Press. (Original work published 1901)

Freud, S. (1961). The ego and the id. In J. Stachey (Ed. & Trans.), *The standard edition of the complete psychological works of Sigmund Freud* (Vol. 19, pp. 3–66). London, England: Hogarth Press. (Original work published 1923)

Freud, S. (1961). *Five lectures on psycho-analysis* (J. Stachey, Ed. & Trans.). New York, NY: Norton. (Original work published 1909–1910)

Freud, S. (1961). The future of an illusion. In J. Stachey (Ed. & Trans.), *The standard edition of the complete psychological works of Sigmund Freud* (Vol. 21, pp. 3–56). London, England: Hogarth Press. (Original work published 1927)

Freud, S. (1962a). The aetiology of hysteria. In J. Stachey (Ed. & Trans.), *The standard edition of the complete psychological works of Sigmund Freud* (Vol. 3, pp. 189–221). London, England: Hogarth Press. (Original work published 1896)

Freud, S. (1962b). Further remarks on the neuro-psychoses of defence. In J. Stachey (Ed. & Trans.), *The standard edition of the complete psychological works of Sigmund Freud* (Vol. 3, pp. 157–185). London, England: Hogarth Press. (Original work published 1896)

Freud, S. (1964). Analysis terminable and interminable. In J. Stachey (Ed. & Trans.), *The standard edition of the complete psychological works of Sigmund Freud* (Vol. 23, pp. 209–253). London: Hogarth Press. (Original work published 1937)

Freud, S. (1964). A disturbance of memory on the acropolis. In J. Stachey (Ed. & Trans.), *The standard edition of the complete psychological works of Sigmund Freud* (Vol. 22, pp. 237–248). London, England: Hogarth Press. (Original work published 1936)

Freud, S. (1964). New introductory lectures on psycho-analysis. In J. Stachey (Ed. & Trans.), *The standard edition of the complete psychological works of Sigmund Freud* (Vol. 22, pp. 3–182). London, England: Hogarth Press. (Original work published 1933)

Freud, S. (1964). An outline of psycho-analysis. In J. Stachey (Ed. & Trans.), *The standard edition of the complete psychological works of Sigmund Freud* (Vol. 23, pp. 139–207). London, England: Hogarth Press. (Original work published 1940)

Freud, S. (2002). Advice to doctors on psychoanalytic treatment (A. Bance, Trans.). In A. Phillips (Ed.), *Wild Analysis* (pp. 31–41). London: Penguin. (Original work published 1912)

Freud, S. (2002). Analysis terminable and interminable (A. Bance, Trans.). In A. Phillips (Ed.), *Wild Analysis* (pp. 171–208). London: Penguin. (Original work published 1937)

Freud, S. (2002). Observations on love in transference (A. Bance, Trans.). In A. Phillips (Ed.), *Wild Analysis* (pp. 65–79). London: Penguin. (Original work published 1915)

Freud, S. (2002). On "wild" psychoanalysis (A. Bance, Trans.). In A. Phillips (Ed.), *Wild Analysis* (pp. 1–9). London: Penguin. (Original work published 1910)

Freud, S. (2002). On initiating treatment (A. Bance, Trans.). In A. Phillips (Ed.), *Wild Analysis* (pp. 43–64). London: Penguin. (Original work published 1913)

Freud, S. (2002). The question of lay analysis (A. Bance, Trans.). In A. Phillips (Ed.), *Wild Analysis* (pp. 93–159). London: Penguin. (Original work published 1926)

Gay, P. (1989a). Sigmund Freud: A brief life. In J. Strachey (Ed. & Trans.), *Five lectures on psychoanalysis* (pp. xi–xxix). New York, NY: Norton. (Original work published 1909–1910)

Gay, P. (1989b). *The Freud reader*. New York, NY: Norton.

Gay, P. (2006). *Freud: A life for our time*. New York, NY: Norton.

Gelman, C. R. (2003). Psychodynamic treatment of Latinos: A critical review of the theoretical and practice outcome research. *Psychoanalytic Social Work, 10,* 79–102. doi: 10.1300/J032v10n02_10

Gerlach, A., Hooke, M. T. S., & Varvin, S. (Eds.). (2013). *Psychoanalysis in Asia: China, India, Japan, South Korea, Taiwan*. London, England: Karnac.

Gilligan, C. (1993). *In a different voice: Psychological theory and women's development*. Cambridge, MA: Harvard.

Gilman, S. L. (2008). Electrotherapy and mental illness: Then and now. *History of Psychiatry, 19,* 339–357. doi: 10.1177/0957154X07082566

Goldhagen, D. J. (1996). *Hitler's willing executioners: Ordinary Germans and the Holocaust*. New York, NY: Knopf.

Greenberg, J. R., & Mitchell, S. A. (1983). *Object relations in psychoanalytic theory*. Cambridge, MA: Harvard.

Haley, J. (1986). *Uncommon therapy: The psychiatric techniques of Milton H. Erickson, M.D.* New York, NY: W. W. Norton.

Halliwell, S. (2005). Katharsis. In D.M. Borchert (Ed.), *Encyclopedia of philosophy* (Vol. 5, pp. 44–45. Farmington Hills, MI: Thomson Gale.

Hankin, B. L., & Abela, J. R. (Eds.). (2005). *Development of psychopathology: A vulnerability-stress perspective*. Thousand Oaks, CA: Sage.

Hays, P. A. (2008). *Addressing cultural complexities in practice: Assessment, diagnosis, and therapy* (2nd ed.). Washington, DC: American Psychological Association.

Hirschmuller, A. (1989). *The life and work of Josef Breuer: Physiology and psychoanalysis*. New York, NY: New York University Press.

Hobbes, T. (2009). *Leviathan: The matter, forme, & power of a common-wealth ecclesiastical and civil*. Auckland, New Zealand: The Floating Press. (Original work published 1651)

Hochschild, A., & Machung, A. (2012). *The second shift: Working families and the revolution at home*. New York, NY: Penguin.

Hollinger, D. A. (1995). *Postethnic America: Beyond multiculturalism*. New York, NY: Basic Books.

Holmes, L. (2008). Why talking cures. *Modern Psychoanalysis, 33,* 71–78.

Hook, M. T. S., Varvin, S., & Gerlach, A. (2013). Why a book on psychoanalysis in Asia? In A. Gerlach, M. T. S. Hooke, & S. Varvin (Eds.), *Psychoanalysis in Asia: China, India, Japan, South Korea, Taiwan* (pp. xii–xxvi). London, England: Karnac.

Hubble, M. A., Duncan, B. L., Miller, S. D., & Wampold, B. E. (2010). Introduction. In B. L. Duncan, S. D. Miller, B. E. Wampold, & M. A. Hubble (Eds.), *The heart and soul of change: Delivering what works in therapy* (pp. 23–46). Washington, DC: American Psychological Association.

Hyde, J. S. (2005). The gender similarities hypothesis. *American Psychologist, 60,* 581–592. doi: 10.1037/0003–066X.60.6.581

Javier, R. A., & Herron, W. G. (2002). Psychoanalysis and the disenfranchised: Countertransference issues. *Psychoanalytic Psychology, 19,* 149–166. doi: 10.1037//0736–9735.19.1.149

Jung, C. G. (1961). *Memories, dreams, reflections* (A. Jaffé, Ed., & R. Winston & C. Winston, Trans.). New York, NY: Vintage.

Justman, S. (2011). The power of rhetoric: Two healing movements. *Yale Journal of Biology and Medicine, 84,* 15–25.

Kahn, E. (1999). A critique of nondirectivity in the person-centered approach. *Journal of Humanistic Psychology, 39,* 94–110. doi: 10.1177/0022167899394006

Kaplan, M. (2004). Psychoanalysis and psychopharmacology: Art and science of combining paradigms. In J. Panksepp (Ed.), *Textbook of biological psychiatry* (pp. 549–569). Hoboken, NJ: Wiley-Liss.

King, M. L., Jr. (1957/1986). The power of nonviolence. In J. M. Washington (Ed.), *A testament of hope: The essential writings of Martin Luther King, Jr.* (pp. 12–15). (Original speech given 1957)

Kitchener, K. (2000). *Foundations of ethical practice, research, and teaching in psychology*. Mahwah, NJ: Lawrence Erlbaum Associates.

Kohut, H. (1971). *The analysis if self: A systematic approach to the psychoanalytic treatment of narcissistic personality disorders.* New York, NY: International Universities.

Lambert, M. J. (1992). Psychotherapy outcome research: Implications for integrative and eclectic therapists. In J. C. Norcross & M. R. Goldfried (Eds.), *Handbook of psychotherapy and behavior change* (4th ed., pp. 143–189). New York, NY: Wiley.

Lambert, M. J., & Barley, D. E. (2001). Research summary on the therapeutic relationship and psychotherapy outcome. *Psychotherapy, 38,* 357–361. doi:10.1037/0033–3204.38.4.357

Lambert, M. J., & Ogles, B. M. (2004). The efficacy and effectiveness of psychotherapy. M. J. Lambert (Ed.), *Bergin and Garfield's handbook of psychotherapy and behavior change* (5th ed., pp. 139–193). New York, NY: Wiley.

Lane, C. (Ed.). (1998). *The psychoanalysis of race.* New York, NY: Columbia.

Leary, K. (2012). Race as an adaptive challenge: Working with diversity in the clinical consulting room. *Psychoanalytic Psychology, 29,* 279–291. doi: 10.1037/a0027817

Lillard, L. A., & Panis, C. W. A. (1996). Marital status and mortality: The role of health. *Demography, 33,* 313–327.

Linehan, M. M. (1993). *Cognitive-behavioral treatment of borderline personality disorder.* New York, NY: Guilford.

Lohser, B., & Newton, P. M. (1996). *Unorthodox Freud: The view from the couch.* New York, NY: Guilford.

Luborsky, L., Singer, B., & Luborsky, L. (1975). Comparative studies of psychotherapy: Is it true that "everyone has won and all must have prizes"? *Archives of General Psychiatry, 32,* 995–1008.

Margolin, L. (1997). *Under the cover of kindness: The invention of social work*. Charlottesville, VA: University of Virginia.

Masson, J. M. (1984). *The assault on truth: Freud's suppression of the seduction theory*. New York, NY: Farrar, Straus and Giroux.

Masson, J. M. (1985). *The complete letters of Sigmund Freud to Wilhelm Fliess, 1887–1904*. Cambridge, MA: Harvard.

Masson, J. M. (1992). *Against therapy*. Monroe, ME: Common Courage.

Mattei, L. (2008). Coloring development: Race and culture in psychodynamic theories. In J. Berzoff, L. M. Flanagan, & P. Hertz (Eds.), *Inside out and outside in: Psychodynamic clinical theory and psychopathology in contemporary multicultural contexts* (pp. 245–270). Lanham, MD: Jason Aronson.

McGuire, W. (1979). *The Freud/Jung letters*. Princeton, NJ: Princeton.

McNally, R. J. (1999). EMDR and Mesmerism: A comparative historical analysis. *Journal of Anxiety Disorders, 13*, 225–236.

McNally, R. J. (2006). Let Freud rest in peace. *Behavioral and Brain Sciences, 29*, 526–527. Retrieved from http://www.wjh.harvard.edu/~wegner/pdfs/Erdelyi%20(2006)%20in%20BBS.pdf

McWilliams, N. (1994). *Psychoanalytic diagnosis: Understanding personality structure in the clinical process*. New York, NY: Guilford.

Mitchell, S. A. (1988). *Relational concepts in psychoanalysis: An integration*. Cambridge, MA: Harvard.

Moncrieff, J. (2013). *The bitterest pills: The troubling story of antipsychotic drugs*. Basingstoke, England: Palgrave MacMillan.

Nietzsche, F. (1974). *The gay science*. W. Kaufmann (Trans.), New York, NY: Vintage. (Original work published 1887)

Ostow, M. (2004). Foreword. In J. Panksepp (Ed.), *Textbook of biological psychiatry* (pp. xv–xvii). Hoboken, NJ: Wiley-Liss.

Park, K. (2011). Asian medicine and holistic aging. *Pastoral Psychology, 60*, 73–83.

Phillips, A. (1993). *On kissing, tickling, and being bored: Psychoanalytic essays on the unexamined life*. Cambridge, MA: Harvard University Press.

Pine, F. (1990). *Drive, ego, object and self: A synthesis for clinical work*. New York, NY: BasicBooks.

Poceski, M. (2009). *Chinese religions: The e-book*. Providence, UT: Journal of Buddhist Ethics Online Books.

Pollitt, K. (1994). *Reasonable creatures: Essays on women and feminism*. New York, NY: Vintage.

Pope, K. (2001). Sex between therapists and clients. In J. Worell (Ed.), *Encyclopedia of women and gender: Sex similarities and differences and the impact of society on gender* (pp. 955–962). San Diego, CA: Academic Press.

Pope, M. (2002). Counseling individuals from the lesbian and gay cultures. In J. Trusty, E. J. Looby, & D. S. Sandhu (Eds.), *Multicultural counseling: Context, theory and practice, and competence* (pp. 201–218). Huntington, NY: Nova Science.

Richardson, T. Q., & Jacob, E. J. (2002). Contemporary issues in multicultural counseling: Training competent counselors. In J. Trusty, E. J. Looby, & D. S. Sandhu

(Eds.), *Multicultural counseling: Context, theory and practice, and competence* (pp. 31–45). Huntington, NY: Nova Science.

Rosenbaum, M. (1984). Anna O. (Bertha Pappenheim): Her history. In M. Rosenbaum & M. Muroff (Eds.), *Anna O.: Fourteen contemporary interpretations* (pp. 1–25). New York, NY: Free Press.

Rosenbaum, M., & Muroff, M. (Eds.). (1984). *Anna O.: Fourteen contemporary interpretations*. New York, NY: Free Press.

Rosenzweig, S. (1936). Some implicit common factors in diverse methods of psychotherapy. *American Journal of Orthopsychiatry, 6,* 412–415. doi: 10.1111/j.1939–0025.1936.tb05248.x

Ruitenbeek, H. M. (1973). *Freud as we knew him*. Detroit, MI: Wayne State University.

Rush, F. (1980). *The best kept secret: Sexual abuse of children*. Englewood Cliffs, NJ: Prentice-Hall.

Schore, A. N. (1994). *Affect regulation and the origin of the self: The neurobiology of emotional development*. Hillsdale, NJ: Lawrence Erlbaum.

Schore, A. N. (2003). *Affect regulation and the repair of the self*. New York, NY: Norton.

Schore, A. N. (2011). The right brain implicit self lies at the core of psychoanalysis. *Psychoanalytic Dialogues, 21,* 75–100.

Shapiro, F. (1989). Eye movement desensitization: A new treatment for post-traumatic stress disorder. *Journal of Behavior Therapy and Experimental Psychiatry, 20,* 211–217.

Shapiro, F. (1995). *Eye movement desensitization and reprocessing: Basic principles, protocols, and procedures*. New York, NY: Guilford.

Sharf, R. S. (2012). *Theories of psychotherapy and counseling: Concepts and cases* (5th ed.). Belmont CA: Brooks/Cole.

Shedler, J. (2010). The efficacy of psychodynamic psychotherapy. *American Psychologist, 65,* 98–109. doi: 10.1037/a0018378

Shorter, E. (1997). *A history of psychiatry: From the era of the asylum to the age of Prozac*. New York, NY: Wiley.

Smith, C. M. (2005). Origin and uses of primum non nocere—above all, do no harm! *Journal of Clinical Pharmacology, 45,* 371–377. doi: 10.1177/0091270004273680

Smith, M. L., & Glass, G. V. (1977). Meta-analysis of psychotherapy outcome studies. *American Psychologist, 32,* 752–760.

Smith, T. B., & Richards, P. S. (2002). Multicultural counseling in spiritual and religious contexts. In J. Trusty, E. J. Looby, & D. S. Sandhu (Eds.), *Multicultural counseling: Context, theory and practice, and competence* (pp. 105–128). Huntington, NY: Nova Science.

Spiegler, M. D., & Guevremont, D. C. (2010). *Contemporary behavior therapy* (5th ed.). Belmont, CA: Wadsworth/Cengage.

Starr, K. E., & Aron, L. (2011). Women on the couch: Genital stimulation and the birth of psychoanalysis. *Psychoanalytic Dialogues, 21,* 373–392. doi: 10.1080/10481885.2011.595316

Strachey, J. (1955). Editor's introduction. In J. Strachey (Ed. & Trans.), *The standard edition of the complete psychological works of Sigmund Freud* (Vol. 2, pp. ix–xxviii). London, England: Hogarth Press.

Sue, D. W. (2001). Multidimensional facets of cultural competence. *The Counseling Psychologist, 29,* 790–821. doi: 10.1177/0011000001296002

Sue, D. W., Arredondo, P., & McDavis, R. J. (1992). Multicultural counseling competencies and standards: A call to the profession. *Journal of Counseling & Development, 70,* 477–486.

Sue, D. W., & Sue, D. (2008). *Counseling the culturally diverse: Theory and practice* (5th ed.). Hoboken, NJ: Wiley.

Sulloway, F. (1979). *Freud, biologist of the mind: Beyond the psychoanalytic legend.* New York, NY: Basic Books.

Sulloway, F. (1991). Reassessing Freud's case histories: The social construction of psychoanalysis. *Isis, 82,* 245–275. Retrieved from http://www.jstor.org/stable/234821

Szasz, T. S. (1960). The myth of mental illness. *American Psychologist, 15,* 113–118.

Tandon, R., Nasrallah, H. A., & Keshavan, M. S. (2009). Schizophrenia, "just the facts" 4. Clinical features and conceptualization. *Schizophrenia Research, 110,* 1–23. doi: 10.1016/j.schres.2009.03.005

Thompson, M. G. (1994). *The truth about Freud's technique: The encounter with the real.* New York: New York University Press.

Turnbull, O. H., & Solms, M. (2004). Depth psychological consequences of brain damage. In J. Panksepp (Ed.), *Textbook of biological psychiatry* (pp. 571–595). Hoboken, NJ: Wiley-Liss.

United States Bureau of Labor Statistics. (2012). *Highlights of women's earnings in 2011.* Washington, DC: U.S. Department of Labor. Retrieved from http://www.bls.gov/cps/cpswom2011.pdf

Vaillant, G. E. (1977). *Adaptation to life.* Boston, MA: Little, Brown.

Vitz, P. (1988). *Freud's Christian unconscious.* New York, NY: Guilford.

Vygotsky, L. S. (1978). *Mind in society: The development of higher psychological processes.* Cambridge, MA: Harvard.

Walter, E. (Ed.). (2008). *Cambridge advanced learner's dictionary* (3rd ed.). [Cambridge Dictionaries Online]. Retrieved from http://dictionary.cambridge.org/dictionary/british/inaugurate

Wampold, B. E., Mondin, G. W., Moody, M., Stich, F., Benson, K., & Ahn, H. (1997). A meta-analysis of outcome studies comparing bona fide psychotherapies: Empirically, "all must have prizes." *Psychological Bulletin, 122,* 203–215. Retrieved from https://umdrive.memphis.edu/mpmrtens/public/CPSY%208200/Wampold%20et%20al.,%201997.pdf

Watkins, C. E. (2012). Race/ethnicity in short-term and long-term psychodynamic psychotherapy treatment research: How "White" are the data? *Psychoanalytic Psychology, 29,* 292–307. doi: 10.1037//a0027449

Watkins, C. E. (2013). Do cultural and sociodemographic variables matter in the study of psychoanalysis? A follow-up comment and simple suggestion. *Psychoanalytic Psychology, 20,* 488–496. doi: 10.1037//a0033616

Watzlawick, P., Weakland, J., & Fisch, R. (1974). *Change: Principles of problem formation and problem resolution*. New York, NY: Norton.

Westen, D. (1999). The scientific status of unconscious processes: Is Freud really dead? *Journal of the American Psychoanalytic Association, 47*(4), 1061–1106.

Yalom, I. (2005). *Theory and practice of group psychotherapy* (5th ed.). New York, NY: Basic Books.

Yeats, W. B. (1996). *The collected poems of W. B. Yeats* (2nd ed.). New York, NY: Simon & Schuster.

Yost, M. R., & Hunter, L. E. (2012). BDSM practitioners' understanding of their initial attraction to BDSM sexuality: Essentialist and constructionist narratives. *Psychology & Sexuality, 3*, 244–259. doi: 10.1080/19419899.2012.700028

Index

About the Author

Fred Redekop earned his doctorate from the University of Iowa in 1997. His clinical experience includes providing in-home family counseling and psychotherapy, providing outpatient counseling and psychotherapy in hospital and community mental health settings, directing residential mental health treatment, and serving as the director of an outpatient clinic. He has facilitated groups addressing domestic violence, borderline personality disorder, anger management for adolescent males, and social skills groups for elementary schoolchildren. He is a Licensed Professional Counselor and a Nationally Certified Counselor. He has taught in the Counseling Department at Kutztown University of Pennsylvania since 2008. In addition to authoring *Psychoanalytic Approaches for Counselors* and serving as editor for the Theories for Counselors series, he has presented at national conferences and is the author of peer-reviewed journal articles, invited journal articles and book chapters, and articles in print and online magazines aimed at professionals and the general public.